7 tools for CULTIVATING your child's potential

7 tools for CULTIVATING your child's potential

zan tyler

BROADMAN
&HOLMAN
PUBLISHERS

NASHVILLE, TENNESSEE

Ten-digit ISBN: 0-8054-4020-8
Thirteen-digit ISBN: 978-0-8054-4020-1

Published by Broadman & Holman Publishers,
Nashville, Tennessee

Dewey Decimal Classification: 371.042
Subject Heading: CHRISTIAN EDUCATION \
HOME SCHOOLING

1 2 3 4 5 6 7 8 9 10   09 08 07 06 05

This book is dedicated to

Joe,

who has taught me to observe life and kudzu

and

who has kept me laughing

through

the death of spiders,

the birth of children,

the threats of jail,

and the lesser crises of daily life.

I love you,

yld

And

to

Ty, John, and Elizabeth,

who have taught me what's important in life.

You, too, have filled my days with laughter (and tears).

There has been no greater way to spend my life

than journeying toward the Celestial City

hand in hand with you.

What a joy and a privilege to

watch your lives unfold.

I love you.

Be there!

let Zan hear from you

If you have thoughts, comments, or ideas on the seven tools, the author would love to hear from you. She would be especially interested to hear your stories concerning how you have implemented one or more of the tools successfully into your family life (please no requests for personal advice). Please send your stories to Zan via e-mail to zan@zantyler.com.

For more information on homeschooling, go to www.life way.com/homeschool. While you are there, be sure to sign up for Zan's bimonthly e-newsletter, "The Homeschool Source." Also visit www.zantyler.com for more information on the seven tools discussed in this book.

If you are interested in Zan speaking to your group, please e-mail her at zan@zantyler.com. Her 2005 speaking schedule can be found at www.zantyler.com.

table of contents

acknowledgments

‹══◆══›

from the introduction to the epilogue, this book covers a span of almost thirty years. My life, our homeschooling journey, and this manuscript are inextricably bound; because of that, there are many to thank.

I would like to thank Senator Warren Giese, who first heard my homeschooling story in 1985 and immediately went to work to right some egregious wrongs. He courageously took up the cause for homeschoolers in the South Carolina General Assembly when there was no political return for his investment, just political fallout. As a former USC head football coach and a Ph.D. in education, we could not have had a more effective champion. Words are not enough to thank him for his integrity and dedication, and for what he has meant to us as a family, especially to John. I would also like to thank Governor David Beasley, Congressman Joe Wilson, Senator John

Courson, and Senator David Thomas for their invaluable leadership in our efforts to take South Carolina from one of the worst states in the Union for homeschooling to one of the best. I also take this opportunity to publicly recognize and thank the late Senator Strom Thurmond for his personal intervention that kept me out of jail and from further rounds of expensive legal proceedings in 1984.

Mike Farris, founder of Home School Legal Defense Association and Patrick Henry College, gave homeschoolers the staying power in South Carolina to remain in the arena to the end. It was Mike's relentless work in the courts that finally forced a remedy for our problems in the South Carolina legislature. When Mike called on a cold December morning in 1991 to tell me we had won a landmark decision in the South Carolina Supreme Court, I could hear the walls of Jericho falling. Mike has been a strong and fierce advocate. But more than that, he has been an invaluable mentor and friend. Mike, Vickie, and their daughters served as our motivation to continue homeschooling through high school. Mike Smith, current president of HSLDA, continues to provide invaluable support to the homeschooling community in South Carolina and around the world. Chris Klicka is a light to us all as he labors to expand homeschooling internationally and perseveres in the midst of severely trying circumstances. DeWitt Black of HSLDA has been an invaluable advisor and friend as he has helped me navigate endless rounds of depositions, law suits, and legislative issues. His ongoing counsel is always reliable and trustworthy, and his friendship is a blessing. I also want to thank Suzanne Stephenson and Grace Matte at HSLDA, first and foremost, for their friendship and also for their professional expertise in producing superior publications.

Ken Wingate has provided constant and invaluable legal advice to us at the South Carolina Association of Independent Home Schools (SCAIHS). Ken's brilliance, generosity, support, and integrity have been a true blessing to us at SCAIHS; but most importantly, Ken and his wife Cathy have become extraordinary and irreplaceable friends during the process.

Since the year 2000, I have spent more time writing than fighting battles. I want to thank Sandy Engel and Rick Reynolds for their invaluable guidance, instruction, and friendship as East Coast/West Coast managing editors for Christianity.com—and for including homeschooling in the mix. My dear friendDr. Terry Dorian has been an inspiration and a mentor, and taught me some invaluable lessons about life, perseverance, and journalism. I also want to thank my young, cool friends from the old Crosswalk.com days who embraced me and helped me learn the Internet culture—Rich Shipe, Jill Bartlett, and Steve and Candace McGarvey. I will always treasure those days together and our friendships. Also a special thanks to Scott Fehrenbacher for his friendship and invaluable assistance.

When Joe and I founded SCAIHS in 1990, we had no idea of the exciting journey that would unfold before us in our efforts to establish the educational and legal viability of the organization. Dr. Steve Suits was chairman of the board for many years while I served as president. I learned volumes from Steve about every aspect of running an organization. Steve's reputation as a pediatric surgeon opened important doors for SCAIHS in the early 1990s. His reputation as a father who rearranged his entire life and medical practice to help homeschool his eight children inspired many, especially me. His spiritual wisdom in some of our darkest nights as an organization and movement gave me strength and kept me going. I also want to thank Dr. Jim Carper, associate professor of educational psychology at the University of South Carolina, who allowed me to freely use his educational credibility in the legislative process when we needed a spokesman with his clout and credentials. John Watson was my dear friend, board member, and legislative advisor. I could never thank him enough for the countless hourshe devoted to SCAIHS in so many varied areas. John has gone tobe with the Lord, and there is not a day that goes by that I don't miss him.

The SCAIHS staff has been my support group since 1990. Kathy Carper, now president, has been a source of encouragement and support and runs SCAIHS with efficiency and sacrificial devotion. Elise Edson was one of my very first homeschooling friends, and her work in developing the SCAIHS high school program has been groundbreaking. Leslie Dixon saw me through Lizzy's high school years, and I am greatly appreciative for her support, friendship, and advice. Emily Lipscombe and Linda Truax are remarkable women and department heads. I'm not sure what any of us would have done without Charlene Witt. I also want to thank the following women: Debbie Humphries, Margaret Poovey, Ruthie McDaniel, Kathy Clinebelle, Jeanne Higgins, Marla Boole,

Nelle Smith, Yogi Wilson, Lisa Sladek, Debbie Essig, and all the other wonderful women who have worked and are working at SCAIHS. Throughout the fifteen years of SCAIHS' existence, my life has been blessed and enriched by every woman who has served on the SCAIHS staff.

I would like to thank David and Lana Waldrop for their crucial role in the homeschooling history of South Carolina as the president of the Carolina Family Schools Association, now known as SCHEA. I would also like to thank Lee Safley for his leadership in SCHEA.

I want to thank my dear friend Michele Steyne, who has helped me on so many different levels, especially for welcoming Ty and John into her home so they could have much needed reprieves from constant visits to the State House when they were young boys. Becky and Gregg McKenzie have given so much to us as friends and have contributed significantly to the development of all three of our children.

I want to thank my friends who have prayed for me through the process of writing this particular manuscript and who have contributed so significantly to Lizzy's life and her senior year: Jackie Hardgrove, Pam Bailey, Gena Antonelli, and Janet Wells. Donna Resseguie and Marnie Drummond have been my Fire Team prayer partners for several years and have prayed faithfully over me and this book from the proposal to the completed manuscript. The following Titus 2 women helped me at critical junctures when I was struggling as a young mother, and I want to thank them for the examples they have been for me: Dottie Aitken, Doris Yates, Gloria Van De Water,

Donna Allen, Jane Simoneau, Kaye Vincent, Mittie Hatch, Margaret Zeigler, and Sylvia Stacey.

I want to thank Jessica Hulcy for the richness of her friendship and the varied lessons I have learned from her, especially about conversation and the way the brain works, and for introducing me to the work of Dr. Jane Healy. Like Joe, she has kept me laughing along this journey. Elizabeth Smith has taught me valuable lessons about prayer and has opened her home to me when I needed a refuge and a break. Tina Farewell has been a dear friend. She has introduced me to new friends, new ideas, and new books. Most importantly, she has prayed for me and encouraged me wen I've needed it most. Sally Clarkson's friendship has encouraged me greatly during the past two years of my life.

David Shepherd, senior publisher for Broadman & Holman Publishers, called me in the spring of 2002 to see if I would be interested in writing a book for him. That call turned into a visit to Nashville where I first met the wonderful Broadman & Holman team. As a homeschooling father of eight, David has a true heart to minister to the homeschooling community and has been working at it for years. My visit about a book morphed into a job with Broadman & Holman to support and promote homeschooling. David's knowledge, expertise, love for God, heart for homeschooling, and sense of humor combine to make this job challenging and rewarding beyond belief. I thank God every day for the privilege of working for David.

I serve as the homeschool editor for Lifeway.com's Web network, www.lifeway.com/homeschool, and the author of the Homeschool Source E-newsletter. Jeff Large, Dan Kassis, Steve Nesmith, and Tammy Wright have been a wonderful team to work with in developing these online homeschooling resources. Their expertise and heart for ministry are obvious in everything they do. The homeschooling team on the Broadman & Holman side of things has been wonderful. Matt Stewart, homeschooling father of four, does things as diverse as working with homeschooling curriculum, developing product, and planning conferences. His heart for homeschooling is obvious in the sacrifices he makes to wear so many hats and help so many people. Stephanie Huffman, in charge of homeschool marketing, has immersed herself in the homeschooling world and has been an immeasurable help on project after project. I especially appreciate her support of and help with this manuscript. John Thompson has been encouraging as we have worked in this new area. Pam Braswell, Mary Beth Shaw, Sharon Gilbert, and Jennifer McAfee have all contributed to the homeschool area of Broadman & Holman and helped me in a host of different ways. I would like to thank Ken Stephens, Dr. Jimmy Draper, and Ted Warren for giving me the opportunity to pursue this ministry that is such a passion of mine. Jean Eckenrode makes my job possible with her invaluable support and encouragement in so many areas of my work. I don't know what I would do without her. Leonard Goss has been my editor on this project. He is the best in the business. I have learned so much from him and his book *The Little Style Guide to Great Christian Writing and Publishing.* He is "boss and bodacious." Also a special thanks to his assistant Courtney Brooks. Kim Overcash, the project editor, is always helpful, encouraging, and on top of things. Kim has been a wealth of help and knowledge to me in many ways since I have been at B&H.

And, finally, I come to my family. In spite of the distance that separates us, my sisters, Donna and Sybil, remain my best friends in life. They and their families have given so much to me and my family. Joe's parents, Mayme and Earle, have provided much support to me during our twenty-seven years of marriage. I am thankful for all they taught Joe growing up and for everything they have meant in the lives of Ty, John, and Elizabeth. My parents, John and Sybil Peters, have been more help and encouragement to me than I could express in an entire manuscript. My mother is nurturing and giving, and has taught me how to teach and how to be a mother by her words, but mostly by her example. Neither one of my parents chose to sit out the homeschooling roller-coaster ride when they so easily could have. Daddy became my lobbyist and chief political strategist, opening doors for me that should have never been opened, using his political clout when I had none, righting many of the wrongs that I constantly encountered, and always offering support and guidance. If Mom and Dad had not stood with me when the world was against me, it would have been more than I could bear.

Ty, John, and Elizabeth have provided the testing ground for this manuscript. They have been great sports to let me discuss them and analyze them publicly. The epilogue expresses my deep love and appreciation for them. Tammy, Teal, and Christine have brought a new measure of joy and laughter into our family.

Joe has been a servant leader in our home, providing stability and spiritual guidance since the day we were married. The children adore him, and I can't imagine life without him. My work on this manuscript, occurring as it did during Elizabeth's senior year, has required him to fill in many gaps—all of which he has done without complaint. Joe's vision for our marriage and family life has defined our home, and undergirds every page of this book. This is not *my* book—it is *our* book.

introduction

Whaen I was a young college student, I used to take great
pride in saying, "There are two things I'll never do in
life—teach or have kids." And so I have spent the last twenty-seven
years of my life teaching my own children at home.

I have learned two lessons during these years. First, never say
never to God; and secondly, being a wife and a mother is a noble
vocation—a high calling from God. I'm grateful that God ignored
my brashness as a young adult and instead led me on a journey
during the last three decades that has been infinitely more
adventurous and interesting than any plans I had in mind at the
time.

I attended Furman University in the '70s. The world was in
upheaval. Headlines of Vietnam and Watergate consumed the
nations's newspapers on a daily basis. Gloria Steinem spent the first

half of the decade promoting feminism (then called women's libera-
tion) through lectures and publications.[1] The drug and sex revolu-
tions powered into fifth gear. Nothing was sacred anymore. The
Bible was out; God was pronounced dead. And liberal theology
crouched at the door of every mainline denomination in America.

God, family, and morality—all were declared defunct and useless in a modern world. College campuses nationwide led the assault.
(Incidentally, they remain generals in the culture war today.) That
was my world as a college student in the '70s.

The Stirring of God

Thankfully, God is never held captive by others' designs. While
the cultural revolution was beginning, He initiated a revolution of
His own. The winds of His Spirit began to blow across high school
and college campuses, stirring the souls of students. Young people
across the country were giving their lives to Jesus in large numbers
and with great fervor. The Jesus Movement had begun.

I had been involved in several Bible studies in high school:
church youth groups, Young Life, and a group led at my high school
by Charlie Schneider, then the assistant principal. One hundred
miles away, Joe (now my husband) was involved in countless Bible
studies, youth groups, and Young Life. Our Young Life leaders gave
us each other's names, and we met during our first week at Furman.

The Christian fellowship at Furman was vibrant. Together, Joe
and I were involved in several Bible studies and fellowship groups.

Then, after being best friends for more than two years, Joe proposed during our junior year. As a college student, I was extremely focused and goal-oriented. My thoughts of the future centered on career options. I had no desire to get married when I graduated from college; I really wanted to go to law school like my dad. In any event, as I mentioned earlier, I knew there were two things I would never do under any circumstances: have kids of my own or teach school. Although I considered myself a serious Christian and student of the Word (for a college student), I had never considered the topic of Christian womanhood. Actually, I had never even *thought* about it.

About the time of Joe's proposal, someone gave me a copy of Elisabeth Elliot's new book *Let Me Be a Woman.* As I read the back cover, I had an uneasy suspicion that my life would never be the same:

> We are called to be women. The fact that I am a
> woman does not make me a different kind of Christian,
> but the fact that I am a Christian does make me a different
> kind of woman. For I have accepted God's idea of me, and
> my whole life is an offering back to Him of all that I am
> and all that He wants me to be.[2]

My suspicions were well-founded. As I read through this book, I heard God's unmistakable call to marriage and motherhood. My life was turned upside down. By the time I was twenty-one, I had graduated from college, married Joe, and was expecting our first child.

In the spring of 1984, eight years after reading *Let Me Be a Woman,* another friend gave me a book that was also destined to change my life and my family's life: *Home Grown Kids* by Dr. Raymond Moore. By this point in time, Ty, our oldest son, had just turned six, and John was three. The Christian school movement was in its pioneer stage, and Joe and I were agonizing over whether to put Ty in a Christian school or send him to public school.

It was in the midst of our quandary that my friend gave me Dr. Moore's book on homeschooling. As I read the back cover of this book, I experienced the same unmistakable feeling that I had encountered eight years earlier when confronted with *Let Me Be a Woman*: I had an uneasy suspicion that my life would never be the same. Again, I was being presented with a concept I had never even heard of, much less thought about.

This time, as I read the back cover of the book, I took the offensive: "God, this homeschooling thing is the strangest thing I have ever heard of. Being a stay-at-home mom is hard enough in today's culture. Please don't ask me to do this. Besides, I don't know one person in the world (let alone my own state) that homeschools. I do *not* want to do this." That was my noble attitude as I read that first book on home education.

God did, in fact, call our family to homeschool, and it has been quite a journey, including threats of jail and years of intense legislative and legal battles. (You can find our family's story in the Appendix of this book.) In 1984, I could have never imagined that only twenty years later, more than two million children would join the ranks of the homeschooled.

So, the same person who said she would never have kids or teach school has spent her entire adult life teaching her own children at home. It has not been easy. It has definitely not been comfortable. But it has been exciting and rewarding beyond belief.

I entered into my life as a wife and mother based on God's call, but I felt totally unprepared and inadequate. Being a mother is by far the most challenging endeavor I have ever encountered. As I have had the privilege of talking to and fellowshipping with thousands of mothers during the course of the past twenty years, I know I am not alone in these feelings of insecurity.

God often calls those He loves to leave the comfort of the familiar in exchange for the discomfiting place of the unfamiliar. After warning him of things not yet seen, God called Noah to an unfamiliar task: building an ark. He called Abraham to an unfamiliar place: the land of his inheritance. He called David, a shepherd, to an unfamiliar profession: kingship. When God calls us to follow Him, He seems to be very concerned about our faith and fairly unconcerned with our comfort and convenience.

Our cultural situation often feeds our fears and insecurities. Today's family has been hit hard and damaged by the powerful force of the culture war that has been raging in our country for several decades. Many of our homes have been pillaged by divorce, weakened by redefinition, and rendered powerless by experts who make us believe that parents aren't capable of anything anymore.

God remains undaunted. He is not afraid. He created the home—He designed it and empowered it to accomplish things that institutions can't.

The Purpose of This Book

The goal of this book is simply that of Titus 2:4: to encourage you to love your husband and your children, and to put some flesh on what that means. In a sense, I have been writing this book for thirty years. This is a record of what God has taught me through prayer and His Word, through research and study, through older women and mentors, through countless mistakes, through trials and tribulations, and through many wonderful days spent with my children and husband.

The shepherds of old encountered the glory of God while carrying out the task of watching their flocks by night. For them, I'm sure that night began like every other night. In the midst of their daily (or in this case nocturnal) chores, they encountered the glory of God, and their lives were never the same. Luke 2:20 tells us, "The shepherds went back, glorifying and praising God for all that they had heard and seen" (NASB). Like the shepherds, I have encountered the glory of God while carrying out the often mundane tasks of being a wife and mother. Christ is present in our homes just as surely as the angel of the Lord was present with the shepherds that night long ago. And like those shepherds, who returned home "glorifying and praising God for all they had heard and seen," so I too want to glorify and praise God for all He has allowed me to hear and see in my years spent as a wife and mother.

I pray that the Holy Spirit will captivate you and speak to you as you read this book. I pray that the winds of the Spirit will blow in your heart, stirring the waters of your soul, and that He will call you to a new level of insight and conviction concerning the absolute importance of your work in the home.

I firmly believe that revival can begin in your home and in my home—in our lives and the lives of our children—if we are willing to hear and heed His call to lay down our lives for those He has put in our care. Even as the world places an unprecedented premium on material success, God continues to focus firmly on relationships: His relationship with us and our relationship with others. In Matthew 9:37–38, Jesus said to His disciples, "The harvest is plentiful, but the workers are few. Therefore, beseech the Lord of the harvest to send out workers in to His harvest" (NASB).

As wives and mothers, our first mission field should be our homes. My goal for this book is to give you encouragement and direction as you work hard to cultivate a rich harvest for God's glory in the lives of your children. Eternity hangs in the balance.

> I've found a Friend, O such a friend! All power to
> Him is given,
> To guard me on my onward course, And bring me safe
> to heaven:
> Eternal glory gleams afar, To nerve my faint endeavor:
> So now to watch, to work, to war; And then to rest
> forever.[3]

chapter one

a vision for preparation, education, and cultivation

Wе have just entered our twenty-first year of home-schooling. This is also our last. Elizabeth, our youngest, has just begun her senior year at home. Her junior year was her watershed year. Her academic load was tough and a bit overwhelming. We had designed several honors-level courses for her, and she participated in a very demanding anatomy and physiology course outside the home. She prepared intensively for the SAT (college boards). And she also invested fifteen-to-twenty hours a week in the performing arts.

In August 2003, at the beginning of her junior year, Lizzy (so dubbed by her brothers) interviewed for an internship position at WMHK, our local award-winning Christian radio station. Bob Holmes, the director of News and Information, selected one home-schooled high-school student per year to serve as his news reporter intern. Bob designed this internship to be innovative and cutting edge: he taught his interns how to cover news events, how to use WMHK's sophisticated equipment, and how to write news reports for broadcast on the air. Given Lizzy's strong interest in broadcast journalism, this situation seemed too good to be true. She applied for and received the position, and all of a sudden we were adding at least ten hours a week to a schedule that was already bursting at the seams.

As Lizzy completed her junior year in May 2004, I surveyed the rich accomplishments and the damage. The accomplishments: She did very well academically; she had an exciting year in her perform-ing arts pursuits; and the internship provided more opportunities and experiences than we could have ever imagined. The damage: Her days started early and ended late. In March she was diagnosed with mono, rested some, but refused to rest sufficiently because of her many commitments. By the time the end of May rolled around, she was exhausted. But like a marathon runner, she believed if she could just make it to the finish line, she could collapse, rest for a while, and regroup. She is a real trooper.

In June, Lizzy attended Palmetto Girls State, a one-week leadership/civics program sponsored by the American Legion Auxiliary. While she was gone for the week, I decided to surprise her by giving her bedroom a much-needed makeover. The year had not only taken a toll on Lizzy's health, it had taken a toll on her room. Every evening for a week, when Joe got home from work, we would eat supper and head upstairs. Joe added built-ins to Lizzy's closet, while I cleaned out drawers, shelves, and bookcases. When we had everything organized, we decided to buy her a new dresser to replace the small one we had bought for her nursery seventeen years earlier.

By the time the week was over, Joe and I were exhausted. We had worked into the wee hours of most mornings to ensure that we would finish the room by the time we picked up Lizzy. Although I was tired, I was thoroughly excited about Lizzy's room because I knew what it would mean to her. She had a busy summer planned, and I knew that having her room renovated and re-organized would be a blessing for her. She had planned to take out several days to deep-clean her room when she returned home. Joe and I were giving her a special gift by giving her those days back—by preparing her room for her. Besides, we had resources she didn't when it came to solving some of her room's space and organizational problems.

On Saturday morning before I picked up Lizzy from Girls State, I took my routine walk. Over the years I have developed the habit of listening to the Bible on tape as I walk for forty-five minutes to an hour. This particular morning I was listening to the Gospel of John. I stopped dead in my tracks when I heard the familiar words of

John 14:2: "In My Father's house are many dwelling places; if not, I would have told you. I am going away to prepare a place for you."

Preparing a Place

Jesus, in His infinite love and mercy for us, has heavily invested Himself in preparing a place for us. This passage took on a rich new significance for me as I contemplated (for what felt like the first time) how hard He has worked throughout eternity to make sure rooms are completed perfectly for each of His children. Just as Joe and I had put great thought and care into designing and preparing Lizzy's room for her, Jesus has perfectly and carefully designed and prepared a place for each of us. Because He is the Perfect Designer, with unlimited resources at His disposal, I know that my room will be perfectly suited for me—not because I deserve it or have earned it in any way, but because my Heavenly Father loves me and has put great thought and care into every aspect of preparing it. Your room will be different from mine—because your Heavenly Father has designed a place to suit you, not me. But we know that the same love that purchased our salvation has been at work preparing our places in His home. If it were not so, He would have told us.

As parents, we don't have had any loving thoughts for our children that did not originate with God. James 1:17 tells us, "Every generous act and every perfect gift is from above, coming down from the Father of lights." Parental love originated in the heart of God, before earthly parents were ever created. We know how to love our children because He first loved His children. We know how to do good things for our children because our Heavenly Father does good things for us. God the Heavenly Father teaches us how to be parents through His Word and by His example (which we find in His Word).

Just as God the Father has thoughtfully and lovingly prepared a place for us, He has placed within us a desire to prepare a place for our children. Obviously, we cannot prepare an eternal home—a heavenly mansion—for our children. Only God can do that. But I do believe we, as parents, are to heavily invest in preparing a place for our children here on earth which in turn will help prepare them for their home in heaven.

Preparing a place for our children obviously involves preparing a physical place—a home. But that is only the beginning. We are to work diligently to prepare a place in this world for our children by carefully cultivating their God-given gifts and personalities. Our goal is to prepare them to fulfill their God-ordained places in this world in relation to their occupational calling, their calling as future spouses and parents, their calling as citizens, and their calling as Christians.

The Process of Cultivating and Educating

Dr. Jeff Myers, president of Myers Institute, is also a professor at Bryan College and the homeschooling father of four children. This summer Jeff spoke at the Glorieta and Ridgecrest Homeschool

Family Vacations. During one of his keynote sessions, he talked about Adam's work in the garden, using Genesis 2:15 as a reference: "Then the Lord God took the man and put him in the garden of Eden to tend and keep it" (NKJV). According to Jeff, the Hebrew word for *tend* is *dabar,* which means "to teach" or "draw potential out of." Then he noted that the root words for *educate* are *e ducere,* which means "to lead out" or "to draw out of."

In her book *Let Me Be a Woman,* Elisabeth Elliot tells of speaking at a Christian liberal arts college. A detractor wrote this in response to her speech, "Why is this college educating women if their primary calling is to be motherhood?"[1]

In a letter to her daughter, Elliot answers the question: "The lady's idea that mothers do not need a college education floors me. What, she asks, is your college educating women for? Surely it is to *draw out* (the root meaning of the word *educate*) the gifts God has given, whatever they may be."[2]

Isn't it interesting how closely linked these ideas of tending, cultivating, and educating are? When we tend or cultivate a garden, we are attempting to draw out of its soil the best it has to offer. Just as a gardener tends the soil, to draw out the best it has to offer—so we are to tend our children. In the same vein, when we educate our children, we are attempting to draw out the gifts and potential God has given.

The ideas of tending, educating, and cultivating are all labor-intensive activities. As with anything that demands hard work, we need to know why we're doing what we're doing. We need a sustaining vision to keep us motivated.

A Vision for Cultivation

The afternoon autumn sun cast a golden haze over the entire landscape as my son Ty and I traipsed through 250 acres of beautiful rural land in the low country of South Carolina. This estate belongs to Ty's friend Norm and has been in his family for more than one hundred years. While Ty finished his last semester of college, he helped Norm manage and cultivate the land.

As we walked together on that brisk afternoon, I could tell that Ty was absolutely enthralled with the beauty of the land, with its assortment of timber, crops, rolling fields, and abundant wildlife. But even more than that, Ty was captivated by the *potential* of the land. As we walked the perimeter of different ten-acre plots, he would point out what he was doing and why, explaining techniques of land management designed to support different types of crops and wildlife. Ty could envision ways not only to increase the beauty of the land but also to increase its usefulness and productivity.

I must admit, when I looked at the land, I saw *land,* not *potential.* I could walk on the terrain for hours just enjoying the scenery and sunshine, but I was a casual observer, not a student of the land. Where I saw ugly thickets, Ty, with the eyes of faith, "saw" paths covered with canopies of trees leading to grassy knolls. Where I saw fallow fields, Ty could envision sod fields, hunt clubs, and thriving crops. To him, the potential and the possibilities were endless.

My lack of vision did not insult Ty. Instead, he began patiently instructing me in how to look beneath the surface and find the signs that tell the real story of the land. First, he focused on the wildlife—pointing out the multitudes of animal tracks indicating the diversity of the species that congregate there. "Mom, these are turkey tracks. I heard so many turkeys gobbling here last year, it sounded like a convention." Sweeping away some pine straw, Ty said, "Look at these deer tracks. Just a few yards to our left, the deer bed down—if you're really quiet, we can probably see them." And, "This is where Drake (his highly trained chocolate lab) and I accidentally jumped that covey of quail last year. It scared us to death."

Our idyllic walk through the countryside was interrupted by my involuntary screams, as I realized I had inadvertently stepped on a snake. Undeterred by my screams or my panic, Ty worked the snake into his lecture: "As the days get cooler, these cold-blooded animals are looking for all the patches of sunshine they can find." He informed me that this snake was also looking for water in the Carolina Bays, depressed areas created by meteor activity that occurred a couple hundred years ago. "You always need to keep your eyes open for snakes in this area, this time of year."

Although Ty forgot to give me advanced warning, he always keeps one eye open for danger. He has learned the hard way to stay on his toes—he has been stampeded by cows, attacked by snakes, and stalked by a hostile buck.

As we hiked back to the 120-year-old homestead nestled in the midst of this beautiful landscape, Ty told me more about the land's potential and how he planned to cultivate it through proper care and development. We also discussed some of the pitfalls, and even the dangers, associated with his work. His enthusiasm, his vision, for this land was not dampened at all by the presence of problems or by his own limitations. He had counted the costs. In his mind's eye, he could see the land ten to fifteen years down the road, and the vision was worth the effort.

During the course of this book, I want to take you for a walk through the landscape of family life. And, like Ty did for me, I want to paint for you a vision of child-raising that is so captivating and enthralling, you will decide that all the toil and trouble is well worth the effort.

Ty taught me not to look at the land only as it is today, but also to look at its limitless possibilities if properly managed and culti-vated. When you look at your children, I want you to see more than the present—I want you to see the great potential residing in each of your children. We'll look at areas of your family life or your children's lives that look like little more than overgrown thickets, and we'll discuss ways to turn the seemingly useless land into useful, lovely terrain. You'll learn to look for and recognize the signs of potential in your child's life that are easy to miss, but are ripe for cultivation.

We'll look at each child's life through the eyes of faith and the lens of Scripture, creating a vision of hope and beauty. We will also look to the Master Gardener as we learn to use the tools He has given us for cultivating our child's potential.

The seven tools for cultivating your child's potential are designed to help you in your planning and labor to prepare the best place possible for your child in this world. They are designed to encourage you in your quest to "draw out" the best each child has to offer. They are designed to point out how God the Father, God the Son, and God the Holy Spirit labor intensively on our behalves as Christians. If we imitate God's behavior toward us, we will be good parents—and our children will have a much easier time believing in a God who loves them and has sacrificed Himself for them.

> Trust in the Lord and do good;
>
> Dwell in the land and cultivate faithfulness.
>
> Psalm 37:3 (NASB)

chapter two

TOOL NUMBER 1

establishing identity

t hat's random." The first time I heard my son John use this
expression as a teenager, it caught me off guard because he is
totally committed to the absolute sovereignty of God. This is the
same son who has been setting the world straight about "luck" since
he was old enough to talk. Anytime he heard anyone say "Good
luck," John immediately replied, "Christians don't believe in luck."
That began when he was three.

I felt compelled to remind John that nothing in this universe is
random because God orders and directs all things—from the falling of
the sparrow to the salvation of the soul. John assured me (without even
rolling his eyes) that this statement did not refer to philosophical

issues, but just referred to anything that seemingly comes out of the blue—like a statement made out of context.

About the time of my conversation with John, the *Seinfeld* sitcom was picking up steam. There is not much about television I enjoy, but I thought I ought to watch this show once just to know what all the buzz was about. I watched one episode, and I didn't get it. I was looking for a plot or meaning or some sense of connectedness between the short scenes that made up the entire show. I was looking for the wrong things. A week later, I read a review on *Seinfeld.* The reviewer made the comment that the entire sitcom is composed of "random, unrelated miniscenes." It is all random. There is no plot.

I have decided that if there is one word that describes the world our children live in, it is *random.* The *Merriam-Webster Dictionary* tells us that *random* means "lacking a definite plan, purpose, or pattern, or to run a haphazard course."[1] Our society is full of adults and teenagers who are random—who lack a purpose for their lives and are therefore forced to run a haphazard race rather than the race that God has set before them.

Today's world is truly random—disjointed, haphazard, lacking roots. Nothing visible is attached to anything invisible. This is like finding the tip of an iceberg that is free-floating, detached from the 88 percent of its mass that serves as its foundation and gives it strength. The tips of icebergs are not imposing, formidable, or strong without their bases. The *Titanic* would not have lost its battle with the iceberg if it had only contended with the tip minus its massive base.

I believe the root of our society's randomness stems from the fact that we have forgotten God. No society can forget God without suffering the consequences as a culture and as individuals. A most visible manifestation of modern society's forgetting God is its almost wholesale capitulation to evolution. When people choose to believe that their very beings are accidental conglomerations of primordial goo, then they embrace the random. When they reject the God who made them, they forfeit that sense of purpose that comes from knowing who they are and why they're here. In a world where even personal identities are random—disconnected from anything with roots we can expect a society with wholesale problems.

For example, in the random world of today, salvation is detached from Jesus. Modern morality is detached from the Ten Commandments. Sex is detached from marriage. Childcare is detached from motherhood. Even education is becoming detached from real life. This quote from John Taylor Gatto, former New York state Teacher of the Year, illustrates that point: "I've noticed a fascinating phenomenon in my years of teaching: schools and schooling are increasingly irrelevant to the great enterprises of the planet. No one believes anymore that scientists are trained in science classes or politicians in civics classes or poets in English classes."[2]

The family has been one of the greatest casualties of our modern, random society. Detached from its scriptural place of prominence and responsibility, the family has become weak and powerless, and parents have succumbed to thoughts that they are incapable of doing anything of importance in the lives of their children. Nothing could be further from the truth.

The Real Question of Identity

In her book *Let Me Be a Woman,* Elisabeth Elliot entitled chapter 2 "Not Who Am I? but Whose Am I?" In our discussion of establishing identity, this is where we need to begin.

From the very earliest ages, our children need to know that they are God's. God created them for a purpose, and He created them in His image. We are all His image-bearers. We bear His likeness. Our ability to think, love, and communicate indicates that we were created in God's likeness. These abilities separate us from the animals. We are not a little more highly evolved than our chimp friends. We are a separate creation altogether.

The psalmist said it quite simply in Psalm 100:3: "Acknowledge that the LORD is God. He made us, and we are His— His people, the sheep of His pasture."

Philosophers throughout the ages have agonized over the question "Who am I?". They have devoted entire careers to studying this question. The following quote reveals a tiny glimpse into the lives of two of the world's great philosophers: "For Camus, the absurd was not negative, not a synonym for 'ridiculous,' but the true state of existence. Accepting the view that life is absurd is to embrace a 'realistic' view of life: the absence of universal logic. This approach to philosophy is more radical than Nietzche's 'God is dead.' One might rephrase Camus' absurdism as 'God? No thanks . . . I'm on my own.'"[3]

As simple as it sounds, we give our children an indescribable gift when we teach them the simple truth, "He made us, and we are His." This gift, though simple, is redemptive. Think of all the time, turmoil, and trouble we save our children when, from infancy, we teach them whose they are. We give them a grid through which to live life. We can save them a lot of heartache in life if we teach them God is their shepherd—they are not on their own, as Camus believed. They know they are not random—they are God's!

The Identity Crisis—Individually and Corporately

According to Jay Kessler, President Emeritus of Taylor University, "The identity crisis of today's young people, individually and corporately, is the largest single factor affecting this generation. . . . [In the colonial era] identity came more from being linked to a family than from being just an individual. A young man was 'the Jones boy' and he knew where he belonged and what he was to be."[4]

Teaching our children whose they are and what it means to be made in God's image infuses their lives with meaning and fills even the mundane nooks and crannies of life with significance. These ideas have to do with each child's individual identity.

Kessler points out that a child's identity is bound up not just at an individual level but also at a corporate level. What does he mean by that? He means that a child needs to know who he is in a larger context than himself. God accomplishes this by placing children into families. "He sets the solitary in families" (Ps. 68:6 NKJV).

The Family—God's Defining Tool

Every family is unique, with a character and way of doing things all its own. This is God's providential design. He sovereignly places each one of us into families to define who we are in time and space. In a day where the importance of family is denigrated—where peer pressure and pop culture clamor to define our children for us—we need to take every available opportunity to provide our children with a positive, lasting family heritage and legacy.

As always, we need to look to Scripture to find God's perspective on the importance of the family, as well as the importance of establishing a family heritage. Once we open the Word of God, we don't have to look far. In the second chapter of the Bible, in Genesis 2:18, we hear this from the mouth of God Himself when speaking of Adam: "It is not good for the man to be alone."

At this point we need to make a noteworthy observation: Adam did not have an empty life.

1. Adam had a gorgeous place to live. Genesis 2:8–15 describes the beautiful garden God created for Adam's residence.

2. Adam already had a personal relationship with God, as evidenced by God's conversations with him. One conversation between God and Adam is recorded in Genesis 1:28–30, where God tells him

and Eve to be fruitful and multiply and have dominion over the earth. Another conversation between God and Adam (recorded in Genesis 2:16–17) concerns dietary and moral instructions. Nothing in these verses indicates that God's and Adam's conversations are out of the ordinary. Conversation appears to be a normal part of their relationship. Genesis 3:8–9 tells about God walking in the garden in the cool of the day, looking for Adam to talk to.

3. Finally, Adam had a career. In Genesis 1:28, God gives Adam and Eve this charge: "Be fruitful, multiply, fill the earth, and subdue it. Rule the fish of the sea, the birds of the sky, and every creature that crawls on the earth." Additionally, Genesis 2:15 tells us, "The LORD God took the man and placed him in the garden of Eden to work it and watch over it."

From the very beginning, Adam already had some of the key issues of life settled. He knew God. He knew where God wanted him to live. He knew what God wanted him to do. With God's blessing of Himself, a beautiful home, and a fulfilling career, what more did Adam need? Was this not enough for Adam? Evidently not. For the first time in the creation account, God surveys His handiwork and declares something "not good."

What is God's solution to Adam's aloneness? He creates the family. It all happens very quickly. In Genesis 2:22, God creates Eve and brings her to Adam. In verse 23, Adam voices his obvious approval. And in verse 24, the terms *father, mother,* and *wife* are used. From the very beginning of man's existence, God—in His infinite, eternal wisdom and mercy—has chosen to place human beings in families. Families are His gift to us—His divinely appointed way of meeting our needs for intimacy, companionship, and identity.

God created and instituted the family before the Fall, before sin entered the world. Throughout Scripture we see God's continued use of the family as a tool to shape and define history. In Genesis alone, seven chapters contain genealogies (or lists of descendants). These are records of *families*. In Numbers, chapters 1 and 26, God orders censuses to be taken of the people of Israel—by their *families*. In Numbers 34, when the Promised Land is portioned out, it is done by *families*. And, after a four-hundred-year interlude, what is the first thing God tells us about Jesus the Messiah in the New Testament, in the very first chapter of Matthew? He gives us His genealogy— His family background.

If God views men within the context of families, shouldn't we follow His example? If God views the family as the foundational institution in society, shouldn't we? Theologian R. J. Rushdoony said, "The family is man's first state, church, and school. It is the institution which provides the basic structure of his existence and most governs his activities."[5] The family is a "framework which extensively and profoundly shapes his concept of himself and of life in general."[6]

The Power of Family Identity

Simply speaking, God ordained the home to be a powerful, life-shaping force in the lives of our children. It is not just a place to change clothes between activities and then crash at night. The home is where children should learn to love God and His Word and where they should learn to love their parents and their siblings. The home is where children should learn right and wrong. Homes should be vibrant places of learning, industry, service, and worship. God created the home to be a place bursting with activity and conversation, while simultaneously providing a place of peace and refuge. The home was chosen by God to be the place where human potential can be energetically and effectively nourished and cultivated.

The home is the child's first dictionary—it gives definition to much of his life. The vocabulary he learns in your home will forever define him.

What Defines Your Family?

Many factors make your family unique. In the following section, I raise a variety of questions to encourage you to think about your family and take stock of where you are. Some of these questions will help you define what makes your family special. We need to celebrate the personalities and gifts that God has placed in the lives of our family members. Some of the questions might strike a nerve. I am not trying to insult you by asking these questions, nor am I trying to make you feel guilty. Everyone has room for improvement. Taking inventory helps us get a more realistic grasp on how vibrant our family life is. Our goal is not to create perfect families. No parents are perfect, and no children are perfect. Our goal should be one of faith working through love to provide a home that is vibrant and engaging, support-ive and instructive, while being characterized by grace and love. This is a tall order, but one we should strive towards. Some days will be bet-ter than others; some years will be better than others. Nonetheless, our goal should be to create a home that is appealing and inviting, a place where our children (and our spouses) want to be because love for God and others abounds. Love covers a multitude of sin.

One more word of warning. Resist the temptation to compare your family and home life to those around you. As I have been speak-ing across the country, I have noticed anew how much women are prone to compare themselves, their husbands, and their children to their friends'. This exercise either ends in envy or arrogance: we want what another family has, or we are proud that we have done better. Neither of these attitudes is appropriate. Jesus makes our priorities clear for us in Matthew 22:37–39; we are to love God and serve our neighbors. Seeking God and thanking Him for His provision for us prevents us from feeling the need to anxiously compare ourselves to our neighbors, friends, or other church members.

Now here are some questions and categories to consider as you assess the strength and vibrancy of your home life.

What is important to you and your spouse? Do you have goals for your marriage and your children? What is your philosophy of family life and child rearing? Is your family life a priority to both husband and wife?

How is your family's spiritual health? Is your family character-ized by love and grace, or have strife and grumbling become more prevalent? Are you seeking to serve one another selflessly? Do both parents love God, or are you alone in trying to raise your children for Christ? Are you actively seeking Him through personal devotions and corporate (church) worship? Do you try to have family devotions? Are your children interested in spiritual thoughts and ideas?

Do you have a spiritual legacy in your family? In other words, are your parents and in-laws, grandparents, and other extended family members Christians? If so, they will bring spiritual gifts and qualities, character traits, and stories of faith to your family that are inspirational, encouraging, and instructive. On the other hand, you might be a first-generation Christian. If so, embrace the opportunity that God has given you and your family to begin the process of building a strong spiritual legacy for your children and grandchildren. In this case, you might want to look to some older couples in your church for fellowship and direction.

Physical characteristics and personality traits often define families. My husband and his brothers, sister, and father all have red hair. They are also great storytellers. Joe has ninety-nine aunts, uncles, and first cousins. Now that his cousins are married and have their own children, the number is more than doubled. Joe's family has a weeklong, family reunion each year in North Carolina. They can sit on the landing by the lake and tell stories and tall tales for a week without taking a break or a breath. My children have been the beneficiaries of this Tyler heritage. Take a minute and think about the physical and personality traits that describe your family.

Your educational choices will determine a great deal about your family. Where your children attend school determines how much time you will have together as a family. If you homeschool, family time can be fairly easily maximized. If your children attend traditional school, you will need to carefully carve out family time in the midst of the school schedules, extracurricular activities, and homework. How are you currently educating your children, and why?

Activities often define family life. Do you go to church together? Do you eat your meals together? Do you enjoy each other's company? Do you read your Bibles together? Do you read other books together? Do you play ball together? Do you vacation together? Do you sing or play musical instruments together? Your family will not do all these things together, of course; but you should have some activities that are enjoyed together rather than individually. How you spend your time does, in many ways, define your particular family. If you have little time together, that is defining. The more time you can spend together in today's fragmented, random world, the better off your children will be. Children need adults speaking into their lives.

Financial considerations provide further definition to your family. Do both parents work (for pay), or are you a one-income family? Do you work at home or in an office? Is tithing important to you? What kind of vacations do you like to take? Are the recreational activities you enjoy expensive, free, or somewhere in between? How much money do you spend on books and activities for the children?

Other characteristics help define your family. Do you live in the country, the suburbs, or the city? Are you politically involved? Are you active in the community? Do you try to make it a habit to serve others as a family through things like soup kitchens, tutoring agencies, or church ministries? Do you travel together or do you prefer to stay close to home? Which holidays are important to you, and how do you celebrate them?

Now think about the quality of your family life. Do you enjoy doing things together? Do you communicate well with each other? How much television do you watch? How do you handle conflict? How do you handle disobedience? Is your marriage strong? Do you view your children as blessings from God, or are they just too much to handle? How are your relationships with your parents and in-laws? Do you have a growing family library?

Many parents today have the daunting challenge of being single parents. This is a defining issue for you and your children. You particularly will need to draw support from your extended family, your friends, and your church family. Remember especially the powerful promises of God on your behalf—He promises to be a husband to the "husbandless" and a father to the fatherless.

Taking Inventory

Take a few minutes now to honestly describe your family, using some of the questions and thoughts provided above. Every family has strengths and weaknesses. Think creatively. What makes your family unique? What do you appreciate the most about your family?

_____

_____

_____

_____

_____

_____

_____

Now think about your goals for your family, as well as the areas that you think need attention or improvement. Take a few minutes to write these down.

_____

_____

_____

_____

_____

_____

_____

_____

_____

_____

Finally, answer this question. Does your family life provide a positive definition and context for your child's life? A stable, vibrant family life goes a long way in providing a positive identity for your child. By actively working with your child from birth to answer the "Who am I" question, you can save him much turmoil later in life. You endow him with an undergirding confidence and strength that will serve him well as he faces adolescence and the adult world. Although the world's philosophers have tried to make this a difficult question, remember it really has a simple answer. Who is he? He is God's.

In your quest to establish a strong sense of identity in your child, remember that he will be defined in large part by the family life you have provided for him. God has ordained for your family to be a defining tool in your child's life.

A Reflection of Heaven or Hell?

Several years ago a visiting preacher graced our pulpit while we were searching for a new pastor. He asked a simple question—What do you think hell looks like? His conclusion for us was simple. Hell looks a lot like the unredeemed portions of this world. It is a place void of God, where individuals lose their importance, their sense of purpose, and their context for living. Heaven, on the other hand, will be full of working, praising, building up, and encouraging. God has indeed prepared a wonderful place for us, and we should be working diligently to reflect heaven in our homes on earth.

These homes will give our children a sense of purpose and meaning. Homes that reflect heaven will be places of positive activity and direction. As parents, we must be intentional in developing this type of home life for our children. Laissez-faire parenting must go. Purposeful parenting must replace it.

Jennifer Roback Morse earned her Ph.D. in economics and taught at both Yale and George Mason University. She currently serves as a research fellow with the Hoover Institution. While Morse's primary vocation now is that of a wife and mother, she continues to write and lecture.[7] In 2001 she wrote the book *Love and Economics: Why the Laissez-Faire Family Doesn't Work.* A former feminist, she says the following about family life:

> When Betty Friedan launched the modern feminist
> movement with *The Feminine Mystique,* she called the

frustration of the middle-class housewife "the problem that has no name." Now we face a different and deeper problem that has no name. I call it "the laissez-faire family." I have lived in a laissez-faire family, and I have learned from experience that it does not work. I was surprised to find that the laissez-faire family, in which each member pursues his own self-interest, does not make people very happy. . . . The proper contrast to the self-centered approach to the family is the self-giving approach.[8]

Self-giving families are those that mirror Christ and His self-giving nature in the grand decisions of life, as well as in a myriad of small, daily decisions. John 10:11 says, "I am the good shepherd. The good shepherd lays down his life for the sheep." John 15:13 tells us, "No one has greater love than this, that someone would lay down his life for his friends." Parents must set the example of laying down their lives for their family's welfare. Children will learn to be selfless and self-sacrificial when they see that quality expressed in their parents' lives. Elisabeth Elliot refers to this as the "exchanged life principle": Just as Christ exchanged His life for us, so we exchange our lives for others.[9] This message is the opposite of the message preached by contemporary society—that we all deserve self-fulfillment. It is in the laying down our lives and giving of ourselves that our homes will most reflect heaven.

How Do We Really Do It?

The work of establishing identity for your child is accomplished on a daily basis as you teach him who he is—he is God's—and as you work to provide a home life that reflects heaven. This will be a home where you actively engage in seeking God; in serving others; in learning, growing, and working together; and in enjoying one another's company. These are meaningful pursuits that breathe positive definitions into your child about who he is and who he can become. As you lay down your life for him on a daily basis, you are telling him that he is worth giving your life for. This creates positive identity.

The following chapters will be filled with practical ways to make your home a rich environment and a powerful place that daily contributes to your child's sense of belonging and identity. In chapter 4, Discovering Purpose, we will delve more into the aspect of your child's individual identity and purpose. In chapter 5, Building Character Through Discipleship, we will discuss ways that parents can use the power of family identity to advocate and open doors for their children.

Let's now move on to the second tool for cultivating your child's potential. In the next chapter we will add breadth and depth to the idea of establishing identity as we discuss ways to build intimacy into your family life. We will see that establishing identity is foundational, but it is only the beginning of cultivating your child's potential.

chapter three

TOOL NUMBER 2

cultivating intimacy

Shortly after her separation from media mogul Ted Turner, actress and activist Jane Fonda said this in an interview with Oprah Winfrey: "Everybody has issues. For me, the challenge is intimacy, but I really didn't start to get that until I turned 60. . . . My big regret would be if I'd never had an intimate relationship. But if you never grew up with intimacy, if you were never with parents who really loved each other, and you never saw that and absorbed it as a kid, it's hard to know how to do it."[1]

Jane Fonda certainly had identity growing up. She, and everybody else, knew who she was—she was Henry Fonda's daughter. But as a child, she never knew her identity in the context of being made in God's image. She grew up in a home devoid of God[2] and, by her own admission, devoid of intimacy. Sixty years is a long time to live without intimacy, and yet it is obvious from reading her entire interview with Oprah that Jane Fonda craved intimacy and sought it throughout her life in a variety of ways and through many relationships.

Unfortunately, Jane Fonda's commentary on intimacy is not unusual or isolated in our world or our children's world. The identity crisis we discussed in chapter 1 is certainly exacerbated by a generation of children who, like Fonda, have never known intimacy. Children today, in our age of affluence and material success, are alienated and depressed. Children experience anxiety disorders and depression once reserved for adults. Placing children on antidepressants, now a common occurrence, was almost unheard of just thirty years ago.

I think the root of this depression is alienation. God created people to live in fellowship with Him and with other human beings. Alienation from God is the primary source of children's depression; alienation from family ranks a close second. For all of its emphasis on achievement and success, this world knows very little about nurturing children and prioritizing relationships.

Why Do Relationships Require So Much Work?

Have you ever wondered why we have to work so hard at relationships? Looking at a garden provides some valuable insights.

Unless the gardener relentlessly weeds, fertilizes, and waters the garden, it will revert to a state of chaos. Weeds will flourish rather than the intended flowers or vegetables. Or drought will dominate and ruin the crops. Constant attention and cultivation are the keys to a garden that flourishes.

Our family has lived in the country for over ten years. Every spring my husband, Joe, and daughter, Lizzy, make ambitious plans for a huge garden. Last year my oldest son even rented a tractor and plowed the land. They begin every year with the greatest intentions—planning, plowing, planting, fertilizing, weeding, and watering. But for the past several years our travel schedule has caught up with the family gardeners, and somewhere in July, chaos begins to reign in the garden. This year was no exception. Once again, because of our travel schedule and the exorbitant amount of rain we received, by the end of July a small jungle had replaced the neatly planned and plowed rows.

Relationships, like gardens, require constant attention and cultivation. Without these ingredients, the weeds will grow out of control and choke them or drought will wither them.

It hasn't always been this way. In considering the family as God's defining tool in chapter 2, we looked at the creation of the family in Genesis 2. It was perfect. Adam and Eve lived happily and harmoniously together, and they enjoyed communion and intimacy with God. And while their garden, the Garden of Eden, required work, weeds and drought were not threats. Gardening was a pleasure, not a painful chore.

Something happened in Genesis 3 that would forever change the makeup of the family. Adam and Eve sinned. In that moment, their intimacy (fellowship) with God was broken, as were their relationships with each other. The image of God within them was marred.

Here is what happened. It's a story most of us know all too well (found in Genesis 3:1–7).

> Now the serpent was the most cunning of all the wild animals that the LORD God had made. He said to the woman, "Did God really say, 'You can't eat from any tree in the garden'?" The woman said to the serpent, "We may eat the fruit from the trees in the garden. But about the fruit of the tree in the middle of the garden, God said, 'You must not eat it or touch it, or you will die.'" "No! You will not die," the serpent said to the woman. "In fact, God knows that when you eat it your eyes will be opened and you will be like God, knowing good and evil." Then the woman saw that the tree was good for food and delightful to look at, and that it was desirable for obtaining wisdom. So she took some of its fruit and ate [it]; she also gave [some] to her husband, [who was] with her, and he ate [it]. Then the eyes of both of them were opened, and they knew they were naked; so they sewed fig leaves together and made loincloths for themselves.

The most telling thing that Adam and Eve did that day was to hide "themselves from the LORD God" (v. 8). For the first time, their fellowship with God—their communion and intimacy—had been broken. This is the most devastating effect of what theologians refer to as the fall of man.

In Genesis 3:14–19, God prescribed the punishment for Adam's and Eve's disobedience. Remember that God had instituted the family and work (tending the garden) before the entrance of sin into the world. Family and work are blessings from God, but when sin entered the world, everything changed—everything fell. For the first time Adam and Eve knew dissension in their relationship. The woman would know pain in childbirth, and Adam would be met with frustration in his work.

The answer to the question "Why do relationships require so much work?" is simply "sin," which results in alienation from God, which results in alienation from each other.

How Can Relationships Ever Prosper?

God is in the business of redeeming relationships—first our relationship with Him, and then our relationships with each other. Even in the midst of cursing the serpent in Genesis 3, God provided the light at the end of the tunnel: "Then the LORD God said to the serpent: Because you have done this, you are cursed more than any livestock and more than any wild animal. You will move on your belly and eat dust all the days of your life. I will put hostility between you and the woman, and between your seed and her seed. *He will strike your head, and you will strike his heel*" (vv. 14–15, author emphasis).

41

In this passage God gives us His first clue concerning His redemptive nature. The seed this Genesis passage speaks of is Christ. Christ is He who will strike and crush the serpent's head. The rest of Scripture—from Genesis 3 through the Book of Revelation—is God's story of redemption through Christ. God has totally and literally invested Himself in redeeming us—in adopting us—so that our relationship with Him is restored. Our relationship with God is foundational to the success of all other relationships in our lives.

The only way we can have good, solid relationships in this life is to imitate God by adopting His priorities and imitating His behavior—thoroughly investing ourselves in those around us. For Christian parents, that means our spouse first and then our children.

What Does This Have to Do with Intimacy?

Intimacy in relationships is God's idea. He sets the standards for relationships, and He sets them high. In Jesus's last recorded conversation with Peter in the Book of John, Jesus asks Peter three times if he (Peter) loves Him. With each successive affirmative answer from Peter, Jesus exhorts, "Feed My lambs," "Shepherd My sheep," and "Feed My sheep." Judging from these words, some of the last that Jesus spoke on earth, we can properly surmise that taking care of others and nurturing them was, and is, a priority for Jesus. When I anticipate my last conversations with my children,

I know I will boil down all of life into my most important priorities—things I want my children to take to heart and act upon. This conversation between Jesus and Peter carried that type of significance. Peter knew that Jesus was giving him an assignment to take to heart—and that assignment involved personal investment in relationships.

In Revelation 3:14–16 and 19–20, John writes the following words to the church in Laodicea: "The Amen, the faithful and true Witness, the Originator of God's creation says: I know your works, that you are neither cold nor hot. I wish that you were cold or hot. So, because you are lukewarm, and neither hot nor cold, I am going to vomit you out of My mouth. . . . As many as I love, I rebuke and discipline. So be committed and repent. Listen! I stand at the door and knock. If anyone hears My voice and opens the door, I will come in to him and have dinner with him, and he with Me."

Jesus does not want us to be lukewarm toward Him—in word or deed. He wants us to love Him, not be neutral toward Him. If Jesus is dissatisfied with unenthusiastic relationships, we will be too: a student is not above his master. As we mentioned in the first chapter, laissez-faire families don't work. Oftentimes, if a child can't get attention through good behavior, he will misbehave. As one of my son's friends told me, "Negative attention is better than no attention." No one wants lukewarmness in relationships. We want them to be active, engaging, and alive.

Note that at the end of this passage, Jesus says that if we repent of our lukewarmness, our reward is fellowship with Him. He provides an illustration of a private dinner, which conjures up a mental image of an intimate time of togetherness and fellowship. Lukewarmness and passivity are the antitheses of meaningful fellowship and intimacy.

What Is Intimacy?

Noah Webster's 1828 *American Dictionary of the English Language* defines *intimacy* as "close familiarity or fellowship." It defines *fellowship* as "communion, intimate familiarity." The etymology for *intimate* is the Late Latin *intimatus,* past participle of *intimare,* which means "to make known."[3] For purposes of our discussion, intimacy means togetherness, fellowship, and communion, as well as the ability to enjoy a shared set of values and goals. Intimate relationships are those in which we make ourselves known to others, and they reveal themselves to us.

The Bible is full of language and word pictures that fully embrace the concept of intimacy. Christ and the church are referred to as the Bridegroom and the bride. Jesus refers to our need to abide in Him when He says, "I am the vine; you are the branches" (John 15:5). He is the Shepherd; we are the sheep. Jesus tells us to remember Him through the sacrament of communion. Even Jesus' name Immanuel means "God with us."

Four Tools for Cultivating Intimacy

During the rest of this chapter, we will discuss practical ways to foster intimacy in your home. For those who grew up in strong homes, your task will be easier. For those who, like Jane Fonda, grew up without intimacy, without parents who really loved each other, your task will be harder. Remember Fonda's words? If you never saw and absorbed intimacy as a child, "it's hard to know how to do it." Refuse to grow discouraged in this important assignment of cultivating intimacy. You don't want your children to be sixty before they experience an intimate relationship. And be assured, they will find counterfeit ways to fulfill their deep-seeded need for intimacy if it is not provided in your home. Teen sexuality, cults, gangs, and drugs are just a few of the ways kids today seek to fill the intimacy void our frenetic culture has created.

The four tools you can use in your home to cultivate intimacy are time, personal presence, conversation, and physical affection.

TIME: THE PRECURSOR TO INTIMACY

When Ty was seven and John was five, I lost a baby girl, whom we named Joy, between my fifth and sixth month of pregnancy. It was a traumatic event that was exacerbated by the fact that I almost lost my life during the delivery process. Because Ty and John were homeschooled, they were very involved in making plans for the new baby. When Joy died, they were devastated. They grieved deeply over the little sister they would never know on this earth.

A year and a half after Joy's birth and death, the Lord blessed our family with a second little girl, Elizabeth, whom the boys quickly and affectionately dubbed Lizzy. About a month before Lizzy was born, Ty sat me down and posed a question that had been troubling him: "Mom, how do you make a baby love you?" None of my answers satisfied Ty, and so we agreed to pray about it together. Ty had been anticipating the joy of having a little sister for almost two years at this point, and he wanted her to love him as much as he already loved her.

When Lizzy was just a few weeks old, Ty appeared by my bedside at two o'clock in the morning holding her. "Mom, I heard Lizzy crying, so I changed her and rocked her, but I think she needs to eat. And, Mom, you remember when I asked you how to make a baby love you? I know. You hold her and love her and help her and spend lots and lots of time with her." As Ty slipped quietly out of the room, I marveled at the simple but powerful wisdom God had revealed to Ty.

We argue a lot today over time. Our new societal mantra regarding child-rearing is "Quality time not quantity time." Have you ever heard the old adage "Children spell love t-i-m-e"? It's true, and there is really no shortcut. Quality time arises out of, not in lieu of, quantity time. I have been a mother for twenty-six years. Because I have homeschooled all three of my children from kindergarten through high school, I have spent a great deal of time with them, individually and corporately. Much of our time together was spent in the uneventful unfolding of life—the routine of household chores, schoolwork, church, and recreation. In the midst of our most mundane days, discussions arose concerning the great issues of life. It is hard to schedule quality time. You certainly can't mandate it with a child. Rather, quality time is something that emerges in the midst of the dailiness of life as you live it together.

The words of Deuteronomy 6:4–7 establish the standard: "Listen, Israel: The LORD our God, the LORD is One. Love the LORD your God with all your heart, with all your soul, and with all your strength. These words that I am giving you today are to be in your heart. Repeat them to your children. Talk about them when you sit in your house and when you walk along the road, when you lie down and when you get up."

As we are engaged in the routines of life with our children, we are to constantly repeat and rehearse the great truths of God with them. This infuses quality into every second of "quantity time." We must remember that the time we have with our children is fleeting. We must be good stewards of the time we have with them, just as we are good stewards of the other gifts and trusts God has given.

PERSONAL PRESENCE

Jesus chose twelve rather unimpressive followers to turn the world upside down. How did He choose to disciple these men for the important mission that would be entrusted to them? How would He prepare these somewhat uneducated men to build His kingdom?

Being the incarnate King of the universe, He had a vast array of training tools and methods at His disposal. Jesus chose to cultivate their potential by investing His time and His presence in their lives for three very concentrated years. He embodied the Deuteronomy 6 passage for the disciples: He repeated God's Word to them in their abodes and along the road, while lying down and rising up. He became the disciples' constant companion. He was with them while they were eating, sleeping, traveling, quarreling, learning, preaching, and ministering. He didn't differentiate between quality time and quantity time. He knew that to experience the ecstasy of moments fraught with significance, He must also share the mundane, time-consuming tasks of life with the disciples.[4]

During His earthly ministry, Christ taught through example, through parable, through hands-on experience, through lecture, and through questioning. Although He made guest appearances to the multitudes, He limited His classroom to twelve.[5] Jesus set the standard for discipleship, mentoring, and teaching when He chose to invest His time and Himself in the lives of others.

In an earlier time and place, God visited Abram in a vision and said to him, "Do not be afraid, Abram. I am your shield, your exceedingly great reward" (Gen. 15:1 NKJV). This verse affirms the premise that God's presence with us is His great gift to us.

Ten Verses Concerning God's Presence with Us

Time and time again, Scripture encourages and exhorts us with the promise of God's presence. As the following ten verses demonstrate,

God's presence with us empowers, enables, comforts, and counsels. His presence is not neutral, but active and engaging. (In the following verses, the emphases are mine.)

1. Deuteronomy 31:7–8. "Moses then summoned Joshua and said to him in the sight of all Israel, 'Be strong and courageous, for you will go with this people into the land the LORD swore to give to their fathers. You will enable them to take possession of it. The LORD is the One who will go before you. *He will be with you; He will not leave you or forsake you.* Do not be afraid or discouraged.'"

2. Joshua 1:9: "Haven't I commanded you: be strong and courageous? *Do not be afraid or discouraged, for the LORD your God is with you wherever you go.*"

3. Isaiah 41:10. "*Do not fear, for I am with you;* do not be afraid, for I am your God. I will strengthen you; I will help you; I will hold on to you with My righteous right hand."

4. Haggai 1:13. "Haggai, the LORD's messenger, delivered the LORD's message to the people, '*I am with you*'—the LORD's declaration."

5. Haggai 2:4. "Even so, be strong, Zerubbabel—the LORD's declaration. 'Be strong, Joshua son of Jehozadak, high priest. Be strong, all you people of the land'—the LORD's declaration. '*Work! For I am with you*'—the declaration of the LORD of Hosts."

6. Matthew 1:22–23. "Now all this took place to fulfill what was spoken by the Lord through the prophet: See, the virgin will become pregnant and give birth to a son, and they will name Him Immanuel, which is translated '*God is with us.*'"

7. Matthew 28:18–20 (The Great Commission). "Then Jesus came near and said to them, 'All authority has been given to Me in heaven and on earth. Go, therefore, and make disciples of all nations, baptizing them in the name of the Father and of the Son and of the Holy Spirit, teaching them to observe everything I have commanded you. *And remember, I am with you always, to the end of the age.'*"

8. Acts 18:9–11. "Then the Lord said to Paul in a night vision, *'Don't be afraid, but keep on speaking and don't be silent. For I am with you,* and no one will lay a hand on you to hurt you, because I have many people in this city.' And he stayed there a year and six months, teaching the word of God among them."

9. Hebrews 13:5. "Your life should be free from the love of money. *Be satisfied with what you have, for He Himself has said, 'I will never leave you or forsake you.'*"

These nine verses are reminders that God always gives us what we need, not necessarily what we want. Sometimes we want things; sometimes we want relief from pain or stress; sometimes we want easier assignments and circumstances in life. God often answers us with His presence instead of granting our specific requests.

Charles Spurgeon, the great nineteenth-century English preacher, said this about the blessing of God's presence: "God promises to set up His tabernacle (dwelling) and His temple in the midst of His people and to make them His priests, His servants, His children, His friends. God will no longer be absent from you. . . . You will be brought to dwell in His presence and abide in His house."[6]

The truth of Spurgeon's words is demonstrated in the tenth verse concerning the promise and power of God's presence:

10. Revelation 21:1–4. "Then I saw a new heaven and a new earth; for the first heaven and the first earth passed away, and there is no longer any sea. And I saw the holy city, new Jerusalem, coming down out of heaven from God, made ready as a bride adorned for her husband. And I heard a loud voice from the throne, saying, 'Behold, the tabernacle of God is among men, and He will dwell among them, and they shall be His people, and God Himself will be among them, and He will wipe away every tear from their eyes; and there will no longer be any death; there will no longer be any mourning, or crying, or pain'" (NASB).

For three and a half years, my son Ty attended Covenant College on a soccer scholarship. During the fall of his junior year, after a particularly arduous practice, Ty suffered from a migraine headache. He used a newly prescribed medication and subsequently lost the vision in his right eye. The whole ordeal was a time of darkness and difficulty for me. Ty, however, embraced his loss with faith and handled the situation with grace. He also wanted to stay in school. During one of my many trips to visit Ty and take him to see yet another specialist, I made an appointment with the college's registrar, Rodney Miller, to discuss the academic repercussions of Ty's loss. Rodney's kindness touched my heart and unleashed a torrent of tears that had been building for weeks. I will never forget what Rodney did as I sat in his office and wept. He didn't tell me to get a grip. He didn't act embarrassed by my outburst. He didn't hand me a Kleenex from across his desk and wait for me to regain my composure. Instead, he rose, walked around his desk, bent over me, and gently wiped the tears from my eyes. In that moment, I saw God, and healing began in me.

God promises to be with us always. His presence is real, eternal, and intimate. As our ten verses attest, He is there to energize and enable the work He assigns us. He protects us and advocates for us. He goes before us and prepares the way. He empowers our words. He is with us in our struggles and labors. He is with us in our victories, and He is with us in our darkest nights. His is not just a powerful presence, but a kind and caring one. His love for us is so tender, individual, and intimate that He even knows when we weep. And as we weep, He rises from His throne as the reigning King of the Universe, bends over us, and gently wipes the tears from our eyes.

The Goal

I often reflect on the cartoon that shows two very small fleas resting on the back of a very large Saint Bernard. As these two fleas receive their sustenance from feasting on this mammoth canine, one flea says to the other, "Sometimes I wonder if there really is a dog."

That's how we treat God. We feast on Him, draw our very sustenance from Him, and yet we question His importance, existence, and abilities. In the same way that we take God for granted, children often take their parents for granted. Their lack of understanding and appreciation cannot deter us as parents from the important task of being there for them. The secular world often questions the existence, necessity, and power of God, just as it often questions the necessity and power of parents. Their doubts and questions do not change the truth. Just as we need the presence of God in our lives, children need the presence of parents in theirs.

As Christian parents, we must understand the premium that God sets on investing time and personal presence in the lives of His children in order for us to understand the importance of investing time and personal presence in the lives of *our* children. Otherwise we will fall prey to secular priorities when we raise our children: we will ignore them or indulge them. In the chapters ahead on discipleship, academics, and leadership, we will talk specifically about how to channel our time and presence in positive ways in our children's lives, encouraging them to be noble, to work hard, and to serve others— just as Christ's presence in our lives does for us. If we focus on loving Christ and serving others, then very likely our children will too.

The Great Commission gives this command: "Then Jesus came near and said to them, 'All authority has been given to Me in heaven and on earth. Go, therefore, and make disciples of all nations, baptizing them in the name of the Father and of the Son and of the Holy Spirit, teaching them to observe everything I have commanded you. And remember, I am with you always, to the end of the age'" (Matt. 28:18–20).

The Greek verb for go in this passage can be translated "As you are going." As we are going about the business of our adult lives, as we are making disciples in the stations of life to which God has called us, we involve our children in our work and our service. Then we can instruct them through our lives that, just as our focus is on serving God and others, so should theirs be. I am not suggesting that we invest our time and presence into the lives of our children to give them everything they want. Children are naturally selfish. It doesn't take concentrated effort to help them become more selfish. We must parent them intentionally, however, to encourage them to be God-focused and others-centered. This is the challenge.

Our goal in parenting should be to mimic our Heavenly Father rather than worldly wisdom. Our children need our time and our presence in their lives more than we, or they, often realize. They need us more than an abundance of things. Our presence gives them a stability, a confidence, and a direction in life that is essential for their spiritual, emotional, and psychological growth. They need to know that we are there. The late pastor and theologian Francis Schaeffer wrote about "The God Who Is There."[7] In that same vein, we need to be the parents who are there.

CONVERSATION

I learned one of my greatest lessons as a parent through a very mundane incident. Many years ago, when Ty and John were ages four and two, I decided to prepare a meal for a needy family in our church. As we approached nap time, my "helpers" were getting crankier by the moment. Like a baseball game that stretches into extra innings and refuses to end, our simple meal was now in its fourth hour of preparation. (Everything always takes twice as long as you think it should with preschoolers.) I realized that by the time we drove the meal across town and returned home, we would have missed naptime altogether. Just as I was tempted to abandon the project out of total frustration, my dear friend Sissy Smith walked into the house.

When Sissy asked what was wrong, I told her that we were trying to prepare a meal for a family in the church, but we had all gotten irritable, things had taken much longer than I had planned, the boys needed their naps, and I was at the end of my rope. Sissy asked if I had told the boys why I was doing what I was doing. Somewhat aggravated, I told her that Ty and John knew we were cooking a meal for a family in the church.

"Not good enough," she replied. Sissy, a teacher who was working on her masters degree in early childhood education, gathered the boys in her arms, sat them down, and began explaining to them exactly what I was trying to accomplish.

"Boys," she said, "your mom is trying to serve a needy family in the church. She is trying to show her love for Jesus by obeying the verses in Philippians 2:3–4, even though she really doesn't feel like it." Then she took out the Bible and read these verses to them. "Do nothing out of rivalry or conceit, but in humility consider others as more important than yourselves. Everyone should look out not [only] for his own interests, but also for the interests of others."

Then Sissy said to the boys, "Ty and John, I know you are tired, just like your mother. But it pleases Jesus when you think of the needs of others rather than yourselves. You are not too young to put other people first. Let's pray now for the needs of this family and ask God to bless them and take care of their needs, and let's pray also that you can serve Jesus with good attitudes even though you are tired." Then we all prayed together.

I learned a valuable lesson from Sissy that day. As parents, we need to carefully explain to our children why we do what we do. We need to use Scripture in our explanations so they can begin to see that our actions, in big things and small things, are motivated by biblical principles and our love for God. This is such simple, obvious advice that I hesitated to share it the first time I used this example in a seminar. But I know from the responses of other women that this simple advice is important advice. The obvious is often easy to overlook.

From that point on, I began to consistently give explanations to Ty and John, and eventually Lizzy, about the reasons for our lifestyle choices and daily activities. I learned from Sissy that day that our children need to see us obeying God even when we don't feel like it. "How else," she asked, "will they learn to obey God and their parents when *they* don't feel like it?"

As a stay-at-home mother, I had spent meaningful time with the boys. That day I learned that I must make meaningful conversation a deliberate habit and a central part of our family life.

The Centrality of Language—Part of God's Design

God is the author of language, and language is one of His greatest gifts to us. Our ability to communicate sets us apart from the animals and is a powerful manifestation of what it means to be made in God's image. Language is the tool that enables us to communicate and fellowship effectively and intimately with one another. From the beginning of time, God placed a premium on verbal communication, as we can see from God's times of fellowship and conversation with Adam in the Garden of Eden. This verbal communication continued through Abraham and others. God gave the Ten Commandments to Moses verbally. Both the Hebrews and the early Christian church had rich oral traditions. The oral vehicle of preaching constitutes a vital part of worship and evangelism today. Jesus Himself said, "My sheep hear My voice" (John 10:27).

These observations are not in any way meant to diminish the crucial aspect of the written word. As Christians, the written Word of God forms the core of our belief system. And that written Word is a record of Jesus, the Logos, the Word of God incarnate. Language is truly central to Christianity. We will discuss the written Word more fully in the chapters on discipleship, worldview, and communication.

In contrast, the pagan cultures surrounding the ancient Hebrews had religions that focused on visual representations—idols that could be seen, but never heard. Images, not language, were central in their religions. Isn't it interesting today that images have, in many regards, replaced language in our culture? As more and more adults and children watch television and movies and play video games, we read and converse less. Even secular research is revealing how deeply a society suffers when it forsakes language—both in its written and verbal forms.

One author says our homes should be "environments bursting with language." Language-rich homes are absolutely crucial for the formation of intimate, meaningful relationships with one another and with God. As it turns out in God's brilliant scheme of things, language-rich homes are also essential for the child's developing brain and his academic success.

Conversation Is Core Curriculum

Educational and neurological research demonstrates that conversation plays an essential role in the child's developing brain and in his educational success. Dr. Jane Healy is an educational psychologist and the author of the book *Endangered Minds: Why Our Children Don't Think.* In this book she devotes an entire chapter to the topic "Who's Teaching Our Children to Talk?" She says, "Good language, like the synapses that make it possible, is gained only from interactive engagement: children need to talk as well as to hear."[8]

The literacy problem in our country may be symptomatic of a larger cultural problem. We don't converse as a society anymore. We place infants and young children in day care, with overworked caregivers who can't possibly interact adequately with those in their charge. Schools encourage silence rather than conversation to maintain order.[9] School-aged children and teenagers come home from school to empty houses. Instead of conversation, their lives are filled with television, video games, and Internet relationships. Homes are no longer filled with interesting conversation. As a matter of fact,

Healy refers to good conversation as a *"rara avis* (rare bird) in homes today."[10]

If conversation is the basis for language acquisition, American education is indeed in trouble. Healy makes this observation: "Dr. Schieffelin, like many others, is concerned that children are not receiving large enough daily doses of talk either at home or at school. With increasing numbers of young children spending time in day-care or school settings, we must pay special attention to their need to talk to adults and to each other, she insists. 'I just believe that kids talking and having language experiences of all kinds, in any kind of medium, is just critical. Kids have to talk, they should be encouraged constantly to talk, and older people need to participate with them, guide them, help them develop and expand their abilities.' "[11]

Christian homes should be the protectors and propagators of language in our "linguistically malnourished"[12] society. Isn't it amazing the rich things we accomplish in our children's lives by talking to them when "you sit in your house and when you walk along the road, when you lie down and when you get up"? Conversation is a crucial component in developing intimate relationships and in preparing our children for meaningful, successful lives.

Conversation Builds Brains

As an infant and young child, Ty had a history of multiple ear infections. The pediatrician never recommended tubes, and I was unaware at the time that ear infections could cause hearing loss or auditory processing problems later in life. During Ty's senior year of high school, I had him tested by Dr. Joel Sussman to make sure he was ready for the rigors of the private college he wanted to attend. One of the first things Dr. Sussman did was send us to an audiologist because of Ty's medical history of ear infections. As I was talking to the audiologist before her exam, she told me she had never had a patient with Ty's medical history who had not suffered some repercussions—particularly problems with auditory processing. My heart sank. Ty has always been an auditory, kinesthetic learner—he learns by talking, hearing, and doing. Since hands-on learning isn't much of an option in most college classrooms, I knew Ty would have to depend on his auditory processing skills.

After examining Ty, the audiologist asked me several questions, mostly wanting to know how I homeschooled Ty. I explained to her that Ty had a strong need for a lot of conversation in his life. If he didn't hear it or speak it, it didn't seem to lodge in his memory. Even into his high school years, we read many of his assignments out loud—together. We discussed topics constantly. He listened to books on tapes—including unabridged classics like *Moby Dick* and *Les Miserables.* (That was a lot of listening.) I had reservations about sharing this information with her because I was afraid that in some way I might have thwarted Ty's ability to work independently (which hadn't seemed to be the case).

After my somewhat apologetic explanation of our home-schooling practices, the audiologist said that Ty did not have an auditory processing problem, and she seemed amazed. She said the only explanation she could give was that the constant conversation in our home had possibly created new neuropathways in Ty's brain, more than compensating for the damage done in his childhood. Conversation is indeed a powerful tool.

I would have to agree with the following observation in *Endangered Minds*: "Dr. Scheibel is personally convinced that interaction with adults, including language stimulation, is one of the growing brain's most important assets. 'Without being melodramatic,' he told me, 'I think it would be very important to tell parents they are participating with the physical development of their youngsters' brain to the exact degree that they interact with them, communicate with them. Language interaction is actually building tissue in their brains—so it's also helping build youngsters' futures.'"[13]

PHYSICAL AFFECTION

Children need constant warmth and affirmation from their parents—both verbally and physically. God chose a very intimate place for a child to live during his first nine months of life—the mother's womb. After birth, the nursing relationship ensures that this physical bond continues between the child and the mother. Fathers and mothers both need to make sure they hug and hold their children as much as they can. This physical affection adds warmth to our relationships with our children and cements the work we are trying to accomplish in their lives. Affection keeps our homes and relationships from becoming sterile and cold.

Conclusion

I worked in the South Carolina General Assembly for many years as a homeschooling advocate and lobbyist. Most of the legislative good that we, as a homeschooling community, accomplished was the result of motivated, well-organized grassroots efforts. I had one bill I worked on, however, that I thought required the help of a professional lobbyist. The first lobbyist I tried to hire, and who actually agreed to work with me, had to renege. Some school boards who were current clients of his law firm threatened to withdraw their lucrative bond business from the firm if this lawyer/lobbyist took me as a client. I interviewed a couple of other lobbyists and finally hired one. The whole experience was somewhat disappointing. I could never adequately explain the heart and history of homeschooling to this lobbyist, who didn't take the issue to heart like a homeschooler would have. Because of these and other mitigating factors, the bill never passed.

Both Ty and John worked in the South Carolina Senate and the United States Senate as pages while they were in high school. Additionally, John worked in the South Carolina Senate for four years in college. During those last four years, Senator Giese, the senator for whom both boys worked, was the chairman of the Senate Education Committee. Because of John's tenure in the South Carolina Senate, he has developed good relationships with many of the senators. In fact, in 2002, one senator who was a candidate for lieutenant governor asked John to stand in for him on a couple of occasions during the course of his campaign. At age twenty-one,

John was speaking with and debating the other candidates running for lieutenant governor and sometimes those running for governor, depending on the forum. It was quite an experience.

John has done more for homeschooling than any paid lobbyist ever could. When approached by senators wanting to know more about homeschooling, John has been able to articulate the issues in compelling and fresh ways. After all, he has been homeschooled all of his life. John needs no long, drawn-out discussions with me over the issues, explaining what is at stake and why. He intuitively understands because he has lived it. A paid lobbyist, unfamiliar with homeschooling, could never know what John knows. Additionally, he understands the nature of politics and legislation because he has been accompanying me to the State House, court hearings, and political meetings on a regular basis since he was four years old.

Several times during the past four years, John has called to discuss various pieces of legislation with me as he sought to understand their meaning and implications. John's grasp of public policy and sophisticated, complicated legislation never ceases to amaze me. On one occasion John called to tell me a senate staffer had asked his opinion on an issue. When John gave me his analysis of the question at hand, I was astounded. This was a public policy issue that John and I had never discussed, yet John's response to this staff person was almost verbatim what my response would have been. At the time I remember marveling at this.

One day, while reading through the Gospel of John, the power and meaning of the following verse jolted me: "Jesus therefore answered and was saying to them, 'Truly, truly, I say to you, the Son can do nothing of Himself, unless it is something He sees the Father doing; for whatever the Father does, these things the Son also does in like manner. For the Father loves the Son, and shows Him all things that He Himself is doing'" (5:19–20 NASB).

Before coming to earth as a man, Jesus lived in His heavenly home with His Father in perfect intimacy and unity. When He came to earth as a man, Jesus could tell us everything about the Father—His thoughts, character, words, and actions—because Jesus lived intimately with Him. Jesus explained His relationship with the Father simply enough for us to understand: Because the Father loves the Son, He shows Him everything He is doing and the Son does whatever the Father does in like manner. For good or for ill, the powerful principles in this verse are being lived out daily in our homes. Whatever our children see us doing, they will do in like manner because they have lived with us, conversed with us, and watched us. This explains why John's analysis of the public policy issue was almost word-for-word what mine would have been. Additionally, this verse implies that one sign of a father's love is that he shows the son all that he is doing.

We need to take this powerful and somewhat frightening principle to heart. We need to be aware that children are parents' ambassadors to the world. They will tell the world what they have seen, heard, and learned in our homes. This is how God designed the home to function. This is the power He has placed in our hands as parents. Our homes have the power to enable or cripple our children—to cultivate or kill their potential.

Unlike Jesus, our children do not have a perfect parent to quote and to imitate. Yet as we strive to please God in all that we do in our homes; as we strive to live with our children honestly, lovingly, and intimately; as we strive to teach them what they will need to know to live responsible, effective lives; and as we strive to encourage them to use their varied gifts to serve the world around them; God can take our meager efforts and bless them—just as He did the little boy's offering of five loaves and two fish. God's presence in our families' lives is powerful and transforming. As we seek to teach and train our children, He is constantly enabling, empowering, and redeeming our efforts, as well as filling in the gaps we invariably leave. God is alive and at work in our homes.

In the next chapter on discovering purpose, we will look more thoroughly into what this means in the life of each individual child. Each child has unique gifts that we need to cultivate as parents. Each will have unique interests and proclivities. Some will be scientists, some will be teachers, some will be politicians, some will be mechanics—the possibilities are limitless. Some will be academically inclined, others will not. Some will be extroverts while others are introverts. God is interested in the work that our children will eventually do in the world, whether it is in the homes they will establish, the churches they will attend, or the vocations and avocations they will choose. As their creator, He has a vested interest in the development and success of each of our children.

chapter four

| TOOL NUMBER 3 |

discovering purpose

$=\!\!\!\!=\!\!\!\Diamond\!\!\!=\!\!\!\!=$

n the spring of 1997, my dear friend and extraordinary artist
Bonita Hamilton approached me about the possibility of starting a homeschool co-op/academy for teaching the fine arts from a
Christian, historical perspective. She told me of a model already in
place—the Master's Academy of Fine Arts in Georgia.[1] The Lord
blessed the idea and the effort, and in September of 1997, the
Masters Academy of Fine Arts in South Carolina opened its doors.
That co-op, now referred to as Excelsior! Academy, continues to
operate and flourish today.[2]

Excelsior! meets once a week, and the core of the program includes
classes on history, art, music, and drama. As the years progressed, we

began adding a variety of electives to the program. I have taught several of these, including courses on public speaking, Christian worldview, and American government.

One of my all-time favorite classes proved to be a public speaking course comprised of a dozen boys, ages ten to fifteen. The boys were energetic, engaging, enthusiastic, entertaining, and exhausting; and since there were no girls in the class, they were also totally uninhibited.

One principle I emphasize repeatedly in my public speaking classes is that stories are infinitely more interesting than sterile facts and statistics. My standard and oft-repeated lecture goes something like this: "Always try to couch your facts in a story for the sake of your audience. While they might quickly forget your three-point outline, they will almost always remember a story. And, if they remember the story, they can almost always trace the story back to your reason for telling it."

I employed a variety of techniques and ideas to drive this point home to my class full of boys, although they didn't need much convincing that lectures can be boring. One day I brought in about twenty-five National Geographic maps of different countries and regions to reinforce the importance of using stories in the context of speeches. I asked each boy to choose a map, peruse it quickly, and share an interesting fact he learned from studying the map. For the first and only time during the course of that class usually brimming with too much conversation and activity, the boys met my request with blank stares and silence. A map usually isn't the source of riveting stories.

Then I asked the boys to turn their maps over. The back of each map contained interesting stories of the people groups that populated the geographic areas each of their maps represented. With this added information, I gave the class this revised assignment: "Read the stories (on the back of your maps) about the people who live in the regions of your map. You will have three minutes to share with the group an interesting fact or story you have learned from studying your map and people group."

With this revised assignment, these boys had more to say than could be shared in the hour allotted to us, and we stayed in our room until the last possible moment, when students from the class following ours descended upon us. When I realized that I had twenty-five very large maps to fold up before I could vacate the room, I panicked. Shane, one of my students, volunteered to stay and help.

To my relief and chagrin, I noticed that in the time it took me to fold one map, Shane had folded ten. As I struggled in exasperation with my second map, I asked Shane how he folded his maps so quickly. I'll never forget his reply: "Mrs. Tyler, you gotta fold 'em the way they're bent."

Our Children's Bent

Shane's insight was simple, yet profound. I was not working with the fold of the maps at all; I was fighting the way they were naturally bent and I was getting nowhere fast. On the other hand, Shane had taken a few minutes to study the way the maps were made, and he was quickly able to fold them because he understood how they were bent. Shane worked with the maps' bent; I unwittingly worked against it. The results were telling and lopsided: Shane folded twenty-three maps; I folded two.

In a sense, our children are like those maps: we must fold them the way they're bent. Pastor and author Chuck Swindoll refers to raising a child according to his bent (his aptitudes and abilities) as being the true meaning of Proverbs 22:6: "Teach a youth about the way he should go; even when he is old he will not depart from it."

Swindoll says, "We might paraphrase the verse to read: 'Adapt the training of your children so that it is in keeping with their individual gifts or bents—the God-given characteristics built into them at birth. When maturity comes, they will not leave the training they have received.'"[3]

In other words, we must make it our job as parents to become serious students of our children, taking the time to discover what makes our children tick and learn how they are bent—so we can work with the way God created them, rather than against it.

The Individual Race

Today the word *curriculum* conjures up images of textbooks or scope-and-sequence charts. But the etymology of the word teaches us that it once had a different meaning. The word *curriculum* comes from the Latin word *currere,* which means "to run."[4] It was first used during the time of the Roman Empire to refer to the course used for chariot races. The curriculum was the racetrack—the course. The *curricle* was the wheeled chaise or chariot usually drawn by horses.[5]

Hebrews 12:1 (AMP) tells us, "Therefore then, since we are surrounded by so great a cloud of witnesses [who have borne testimony to the Truth], let us strip off and throw aside every encumbrance (unnecessary weight) and that sin which so readily (deftly and cleverly) clings to and entangles us, and let us run with patient endurance and steady and active persistence the appointed course of the race that is set before us."

Each child has a different course—a different curriculum—that has been set before him. Who is the one who has set this appointed course before him? It is, of course, God. As parents, we should do everything in our power to enable each child to successfully navigate and complete the race that God has given him to run.

Remember our conversation in chapter 2 about establishing identity? We talked about the random nature of our society. We defined *random* as "lacking a definite plan, purpose, or pattern, or to run a haphazard course." This idea of a random or haphazard course stands in direct opposition to the Christian notion of life. We nor our children run a haphazard course; we run the appointed course that God has set before us. This gives immediate and lasting meaning and purpose to our lives as individuals. We are God's. He is our creator, and He is the curriculum (course) designer for each of us and each of our children.

Maintaining an Eternal Perspective

Before we begin our discussion of practical ways to help your child discover his particular course and purpose in life, I want us to consider together some of the dilemmas and difficulties of being parents. If you know realistically what to expect as you earnestly seek to raise your children for Christ and as you work at cultivating their potential, you can more easily and successfully navigate the sometimes difficult landscape of family life.

During the years when your children are home and all-consuming, the pace of life can become hectic and frenetic. Household responsibilities, coupled with the desire to provide the best for your child in every realm of his life, can put overwhelming pressure on you. Add to that the frustrating facts that every parent and every child are imperfect, and parenting, unfortunately, cannot be reduced to a simple formula. What works with one child might fail miserably with another. If we don't maintain an eternal perspective in this exhilarating and exhausting adventure of raising our children, we will be tempted to give up and take the laissez-faire way out.

For many years I recited the following words of Paul to myself on a daily basis: "Don't be deceived: God is not mocked. For whatever a man sows he will also reap, because the one who sows to his flesh will reap corruption from the flesh, but the one who sows to the Spirit will reap eternal life from the Spirit. *So we must not get tired of doing good, for we will reap at the proper time if we don't give up. Therefore, as we have opportunity, we must work for the good of all, especially for those who belong to the household of faith"* (Gal. 6:7–10, author emphasis).

These verses helped me maintain an eternal perspective and purpose as I labored over my children. (Sowing is hard work!) I had to constantly remind myself not to grow tired and give up in the process of working for the good of my children. Sometimes in the midst of our most back-breaking labor, we see no visible results. In those times, we must remember to walk by faith, not by sight. Again, Paul's words encourage us: "Therefore we do not give up; even though our outer person is being destroyed, our inner person is being renewed day by day. For our momentary light affliction is producing for us an absolutely incomparable eternal weight of glory. So we do not focus on what is seen, but on what is unseen; for what is seen is temporary, but what is unseen is eternal" (2 Cor. 4:16–18).

Much of our work as parents is devoted to developing a strong, undergirding root system for our children that will provide strength and nourishment to them throughout their lives. The fact that these roots are invisible doesn't mean they aren't vital to our children's success, but it does mean we often can't see the results of our labor. Almost all roots are invisible to the human eye.

Isaiah 37:31 says, "The surviving remnant of the house of Judah will again take root downward and bear fruit upward."

This verse emphasizes the principle that growing a strong root system is essential in cultivating our children's potential. Our children need strong roots to enable them to bear abundant fruit as they grow and mature. To bear fruit upward as they grow older and more mature, they must first take root downward. This invisible aspect of developing deep roots is perhaps our greatest, and most difficult, task as parents.

The world around us often doesn't have eyes to see the essential root-developing work that is taking place on a daily basis in our homes. Our society likes to measure success in terms of quantifiable outcomes. For parents, that means that all too often we allow our effectiveness to be defined by outward measures in our children, such as good behavior and academic success. Good behavior and good grades are certainly not bad things, but they will be somewhat meaningless if we have failed to develop the inner life, the under-ground root system, of the child. We must constantly remind our-selves to focus on the unseen in our materialistic world, because the unseen has eternal significance.

We have to get the order right for our children to enjoy abun-dant and productive lives. They must first have roots that grow downward before they can bear meaningful fruit upward. If we focus on outward behavior, grades, and accomplishments without first focusing on the invisible root system, we are setting our children up for trouble. At best, they will lead shallow lives based on outward accomplishments. What happens to them when things go wrong and they are faced with trials and tribulations—or even worse—failure? They will have no reliable root system to sustain and nourish them during these times of drought, which every human being inevitably encounters. At worst, by allowing ourselves and our children to focus on outward measures of success only, we are dooming them to lives that will be void of intrinsic meaning and purpose, setting the stage for emotional or psychological problems later in life caused by this relentless pursuit of success.

We discussed the philosopher Camus in chapter 2. He experienced academic success, but a confused life. Today's world has witnessed a renaissance of smart people with little underlying character. We must remember, however, that even good behavior can be a shallow measure of success if it is not predicated on a root system that has been carefully cultivated. Moralism and Christianity are not one in the same. Our salvation as Christians is based on faith, not works. When we work hard to cultivate our children's potential in the invisible realms of life before we focus on outward behavior and success, we are giving our children every opportunity to live full and meaningful lives. When our children know who they are, when they have intimate relationships with God and with others, and when they can appreciate their individual gifts and strengths, they possess a robust root system of invisible qualities that will allow them to "bear fruit upward" and to weather the inevitable storms of life. (In chapters 6 through 8 we will begin to discuss this visible fruit.)

We must remind ourselves daily not to grow tired and give up in this important labor of child-rearing. We have to constantly remember to focus on the unseen rather than the seen, the eternal rather than the temporal. Then we can run with endurance "the appointed course of the race that is set before us" as parents. As our children see us run with endurance and perseverance, it will encourage them to do the same.

Now we can resume our discussion of practical ways to help your child discover his particular course and purpose in life.

Beginning the Journey of Discovery

To help our children discern and travel God's course for them, to help them begin to discover who they are and how they are bent, we must commit to the following four actions.

1. We must seek God and pray for our children on a regular basis. We need God's continued wisdom, insight, and help if we are to understand how He has created each of our children—what particular bent He has given to each.

2. We must agree to devote the time and energy it takes to study and observe our children so we can more fully understand each child's unique personality, gifts, interests, strengths, and weaknesses. Chuck Swindoll emphasizes the importance of taking the time to become students of our children: "Give your child the time it takes to find out how he or she is put together. Help your child know who he or she is. Help them know themselves so that they learn to love and accept themselves as they are. Then as they move into a society that seems committed to pounding them into another shape, they will remain true to themselves, secure in their independent walk with their God. I have begun to realize that secure, mature people are best described in fifteen words. They know who they are . . . they like who they are . . . they are who they are. They are *real*."[6]

3. We must be willing to accept and affirm each child, along with his strengths and weaknesses. We cannot try to make our son or our daughter into something he or she is not. Remember, we must "fold 'em the way they're bent" (the way God bent them), rather than fight against the bent. Some children will be academically gifted; others will be learning disabled. Some will be athletic; others will be clumsy. Some will be musical, while others will be tone deaf. Some will be naturally quiet and compliant, while others will be active and loudly inquisitive.

4. We must be willing to come alongside our children to help them, guide them, and cheer them on. This guidance includes correction and discipline, to be sure; but even this should be offered in an attitude that re-affirms our commitment to work alongside our children, helping them to "strip off and throw aside every encumbrance and that sin which so readily clings to and entangles" them, enabling them to effectively run the race that God has set before them.

In a chapter entitled "Discarding Unbiblical Methods" (of discipline), Ted Tripp, author of *Shepherding a Child's Heart,* discusses a number of poor choices parents make when disciplining their children. In the context of this conversation, he discusses grounding. For our purposes, the point here is not really to debate the pros and cons of grounding, but to reinforce the notion that even our discipline is for the child's sake: "The problem here is that none of the issues that caused the poor behavior for which he is grounded are being addressed. . . . *You see, grounding is not designed to do something for the child; it is designed to do something against him.* Grounding is not corrective. It is simply punitive. . . . It doesn't require ongoing interaction. It does not require ongoing discussion. It does not assess what is going on inside the child. It does not require patient instruction and entreaty"[7] (author emphasis). Even our correction should be redemptive. It should lead the child to repentance and to Christ.

Three Diagnostic Questions for the Journey

In November 1995, I received an invitation from Dr. Barbara Nielsen, South Carolina Superintendent of Education, to attend a workshop hosted by the State Department of Education entitled "Education and Technology." At the time, I was serving as president of the South Carolina Association of Independent Home Schools (SCAIHS), a homeschooling organization my husband and I founded in July 1990.[8]

In 1995, people were beginning to talk about the Internet, but I certainly had no understanding of it. I was not alone—most of the educators at the conference seemed to have little more knowledge than I did about the World Wide Web. (Now, just ten years later, it is hard to even imagine that.) After listening to the keynote sessions, attendees could choose from a number of breakout sessions that were offered on various aspects of technology in education. I opted for a workshop presented by Dr. Larry S. Rosen, professor of educational psychology at Stetson University, analyzing and discussing the Celebration School and Teaching Academy.

In this breakout session, Dr. Rosen told the story of how Stetson University, the Osceola (Florida) Public School District, and the Disney Development Corporation in Orlando, Florida, came together to develop an "exemplary" school for kindergarten through grade twelve. This is the synopsis I wrote at the time based on my notes from the session and the handouts I received:

> This planned community developed by the Disney Development Corporation in Orlando, Florida, includes an "exemplary" school with technology linkages to the community and beyond. The academy, when it opens in August, will promote exemplary practices in education by modeling and implementing state-of-the-art technology, educational research, training, and curriculum. In typical Disney fashion, no expense was spared (millions were spent) in bringing in the greatest educational minds in the country to develop what is considered the brightest and best school system in the country. It was encouraging to me to realize that many of their educational tenets are cornerstones in the home education lifestyle (small classes with a variety of ages; varied subjects taught together; flexible scheduling to promote maximum learning; learning areas with sofas and chairs rather than desks lined in a row; and active, sometimes noisy, environments). One of the cornerstones of their educational philosophy is the development of "personalized learning plans" for each and

every student—not just the learning disabled or gifted.
Sure sounds like home schooling to me.

I remember Dr. Rosen saying that in order to determine this
personalized learning plan for each student, teachers would need to
ask the following questions about each student. (The words in paren-
theses are mine.)

- Where is he "at";
- Where does he want to go (or what does he want to do in life);
  and
- How can he get there (and how can we help guide him)?

Our homes are perfectly designed forums for asking these questions and for developing incredibly powerful personalized learning
plans for each child. We should constantly ask these questions about
each of our children. These questions are appropriate not only for our
developing our children's educational endeavors but they also are
helpful in assessing our children's spiritual growth and gifts, their
personality types, and their strengths and weaknesses.

The three questions are essential and effective because they can
help keep us focused on the right things. We should always be looking at the long-term goal of getting each child where he should be
in life—of helping him successfully navigate and complete the
course that God has set before him.

Five Tools for Discovering Purpose

To know God and bring glory to Him is every child's over-arching purpose; to discover God and glorify Him within the context of the race that God has set before him defines the child's individual purpose. During the rest of this chapter we will discuss practical ways that you, as parents, can help your children in this process of discovering individual purpose. We will discuss five areas in particular: loving your child unconditionally, nurturing his spiritual growth and gifts, understanding his basic personality, determining his learning style(s), and discovering his strengths. Armed with this knowledge, you can prayerfully and purposely design a lifestyle and an educational plan that will cultivate your child's potential—that will "draw out" the best he has to offer to God, his family, his church, and his community. As you read through the following pages, ask the three diagnostic questions often about your children. Keep a notebook or journal by your side as you read so you can record your observations about each child.

LOVING YOUR CHILD UNCONDITIONALLY

We must be willing to love and affirm our children as God created them, not as we wish He had created them. This bears repeating: We must be willing to love and affirm our children as God created them, not as we wish He had created them. Gary Chapman, Ph.D., and Ross Campbell, M.D., authors of *The Five Love Languages of Children,* express it this way:

> Every child has an emotional tank, a place of emo-
> tional strength that can fuel him through the challenging
> days of childhood and adolescence. Just as cars are powered
> by reserves in the gas tank, our children are fueled by their
> emotional tanks. We must fill our children's emotional
> tanks for them to operate as they should and reach their
> potential. But with what do we fill these tanks? Love, of
> course, but love of a particular kind that will enable our
> children to grow and function properly.
>
> We need to fill our children's tanks with *unconditional*
> love, because real love is always unconditional.
> Unconditional love is a full love that accepts and affirms
> a child for who he is, not for what he does. No matter
> what he does (or does not do), the parent still loves him.
> Sadly, parents often display a love that is conditional: it
> depends on something other than their children just
> being.[9]

Love—biblical, sacrificial, unconditional love—resides at the very core of meaningful, positive relationships. First Corinthians 13:4–8 describes some of the characteristics of this type of love. "Love is patient; love is kind. Love does not envy; is not boast-ful; is not conceited; does not act improperly; is not selfish; is not provoked; does not keep a record of wrongs; finds no joy in unrighteousness, but rejoices in the truth; bears all things, believes all things, hopes all things, endures all things. Love never ends."

My husband, Joe, has always made our three children a top priority in his life. He has loved them and sacrificed for them in a myriad of ways—both large and small. When Ty and John were little boys, he gave up activities he would have normally enjoyed pursuing on Saturdays (golf, hunting, and fishing) to be with them. When Joe was home and the boys were awake, they were engaged in activities together. Joe always said that when he came home from work, he was coming home to his most important job—being a good husband and father. He never came home expecting to be able to relax on the sofa while life continued around him.

As a result of Joe's total devotion to the boys (and Lizzy, who came along seven years after John), they were and are totally devoted to him. I can remember times when Joe would tell the boys he needed to be out of town due to work commitments. They would throw themselves on the floor and cry as if their little hearts might break. These childish expressions of their total love for their dad were sometimes accompanied by more profound moments.

One Sunday morning, after a particularly tiring Saturday, we were all in church. John, who was five years old at the time, leaned over to ask me a question. "Mom," he whispered much too loudly, "what's bothering Daddy?" I looked over at Joe, who was sound asleep as the pastor preached on.

I drew John close and whispered back to him, "I think Dad is really OK; why do you think something is bothering him?"

Then John whispered again, "Because, Mom, he is deep in prayer about something."

We should all love our children like John loves his dad. When we look at them through the lens of 1 Corinthians 13, we will bear all things, believe all things, hope all things, endure all things. When we look at someone through the eyes of unconditional love, we will see their potential and believe and hope for the best in their lives. When John looked at his dad through the eyes of love, he automatically assumed the best: Joe was praying, not sleeping. This type of love should be our default setting for our children.

The Power of Affirmation

My mother was an extraordinarily effective fourth-grade school teacher. She is five feet tall, weighs one hundred pounds, and has always been soft-spoken and optimistic, both at home and at school. In spite of her diminutive size, the principal always gave her the toughest boys. By the end of every school year, my tiny, soft-spoken mother would have every roughneck boy under control. She rarely had discipline problems in her classroom.

One day I asked Mom how she did it. Her methods were simple but profound and powerful. Before the beginning of every school year, she received permanent records on all of her students. She refused to read any of these until after she had taught each student for six weeks and had issued each one his first report card of the school year. Instead of reading what previous teachers had thought of each child, she wanted to form her own opinions. She started every school year assuming the best about each child. She assumed that each student would try hard and behave well, and she communicated that constantly to her class.

Some of her students had probably never had a positive thought expressed about them in their lives. My mother found a way to praise and encourage every student in her class, and this was in the days of thirty-five and forty students in a classroom. She worked hard at affirming her students. Although she never showed it, I know there had to have been days and students that discouraged her. But she really wanted each of her students to succeed.

Mom had realistic expectations. She didn't expect all of her students to make As, but she did expect them to do the best they could. She treated her C students with the same respect she gave her A students. She never raised her voice in the classroom. When things got a little too rowdy or noisy, she would begin whispering.

Mom's simple prescription of setting high (behavioral) expectations, expressing constant affirmation, and believing in her students produced remarkable results year after year in the lives of her students.

We can implement these same standards in our homes. Our children need to be constantly reminded that we love them, respect them, and believe in them.

The Crippling Power of Negativity

We tend to believe what we are told about ourselves if it is repeated and reinforced enough. My parents loved and affirmed me.

My dad always told me I could do anything I set my mind to. I believed him. My goal-driven nature pushed me to succeed in school; I did well and received positive feedback and reinforcement about my academic pursuits. Positive expectations and affirmation breed success.

I am five feet tall. That's it. My mother and two sisters are also five feet tall. Even though I have been this height for as long as I can remember, I never thought of myself as short until my daughter, Lizzy, was five-years-old. Ty was fourteen and John was twelve; both boys were at least eight inches taller than I was at this point in time. Every morning when Lizzy came downstairs for breakfast, she would make a point of asking Ty, John, and me to stand together. Then she would make the same pronouncement each morning: "Mom, you are short." This continued for almost a year. One morning I had been asked to testify at a legislative hearing on homeschooling. As I entered the hearing room at the State House, I surveyed the senators who were present and the others who would be testifying, and for the first time in my life thought, *I'm short.*

I know this story sounds a little ridiculous, because everyone else in the world realizes I am short. But I had never thought about my height in terms of it being a liability until Lizzy pointed it out on a daily basis. If my sweet little five-year-old daughter could cause this change in my perspective, think about the crippling influence parents exert when they choose to point out and constantly focus on the negative aspects of a child's personality, physical appearance, or academic abilities.

Not until I was an adult did I encounter a situation where someone questioned my abilities and motives. It was a demoralizing and
depressing experience for me, and it took me quite a bit of time to
recover emotionally from it. I wonder how children survive who are
fed a constant diet of criticism and complaints during their formative childhood years. It must exact a heavy toll on them. I often
hear speakers who confess to being starved of parental approval
and affirmation (especially from their fathers). They tell heart-
wrenching stories of spending their entire adult lives trying to gain
their fathers' approval.

Being committed to unconditional love and constant affirmation does not mean we condone or excuse bad behavior in our children. We must address unacceptable behavior as it occurs. But the
child who is constantly loved and affirmed will generally need less
correction than a child who has been ignored or constantly criticized.
Sometimes bad behavior is a child's way of crying out for some sort
of attention. Dr. Chapman and Dr. Campbell say this about discipline: "Of course, it is necessary to train and/or discipline our children—but only after their emotional tanks have been filled. Those
tanks can be filled with only one premium fuel: unconditional love.
Our children have 'love tanks' ready to be filled (and refilled; they
can deplete regularly). Only unconditional love can prevent problems such as resentment, feelings of being unloved, guilt, fear, and
insecurity. Only as we give our children unconditional love will we
be able to deeply understand them and deal with their behaviors,
whether good or bad."[10]

Children, by and large, will believe what parents tell them about themselves. Remember from our discussion in chapter 2 on establishing identity that families have great defining power in the lives of children? We must be good stewards of this power and trust that which God has placed in our hands. We enable our children by voicing our affirmation and love for them. We can cripple them by constantly criticizing, berating, and questioning them. This is not an empty "power of positive thinking" mentality or a "name it and claim it" scheme. When we thoughtfully study our children and have a good grasp of who they are, we can find many ways to affirm, love, and encourage them.

NURTURING YOUR CHILD'S SPIRITUAL GROWTH AND GIFTS

In chapter 1 of this book, we discussed the importance of preparing a place for our children. In chapter 2, we considered the idea that our homes should be reflections of heaven, where meaningful pursuits abound. In chapter 3 we delved into the importance of developing intimacy with our children through investing our time and personal presence in their lives, as well as through engaging in constant conversation with them.

If, in conjunction with these things, we are making God the focal point of life in our homes, we will be creating atmospheres for our children that nurture and support their spiritual growth. Family devotions and church involvement add some formalized training and direction to our children's spiritual lives. In the next chapter, on developing worldview, we will discuss very specific ways to train children to think and act as Christians in a non-Christian world.

As our children grow up in environments that foster their faith, their spiritual gifts will begin to emerge. Every Christian has been given spiritual gifts. *The Holman Bible Dictionary* defines spiritual gifts as "The skills and abilities which God gives through His Spirit to all Christians, which equip Christians to serve God in the Christian community."[11]

Many lists of specific spiritual gifts are given in the Bible. We will record a few here, but this is not meant to be a comprehensive account by any stretch of the imagination. Many books have been written on the topic of spiritual gifts, and it would impossible to adequately treat this subject in the small amount of space we have here. This section is designed to prompt you to think about and encourage the gifts and growth you see in each individual child.

Information Concerning Spiritual Gifts

Romans 12:6–8 tells us the following: "According to the grace given to us, we have different gifts: If prophecy, use it according to the standard of faith; if service, in service; if teaching, in teaching; if exhorting, in exhortation; giving, with generosity; leading, with diligence; showing mercy, with cheerfulness."

Ephesians 4:11–13 supplies more information: "And He personally gave some to be apostles, some prophets, some evangelists, some pastors and teachers, for the training of the saints in the work of ministry, to build up the body of Christ, until we all reach unity in the faith and in the knowledge of God's Son, [growing] into a mature man with a stature measured by Christ's fullness."

First Corinthians 12:4–7 gives this information about gifts: "Now there are different gifts, but the same Spirit. There are different ministries, but the same Lord. And there are different activities, but the same God is active in everyone and everything. A manifestation of the Spirit is given to each person to produce what is beneficial."

The Holman Bible Dictionary furnishes this final bit of insight for us: "Some Christians today tend to want to distinguish spiritual gifts from natural abilities, but this distinction seems not to have occurred to Paul, for he included both in his lists (see, for example, Romans 12:6–8). His assumption seems to have been that *whatever skills a Christian has are given to him by God and are to be used in God's service. What matters, then, is that Christians discover what their gifts are and then develop them*" (author emphasis).[12]

This information makes it clear that our goal as parents is threefold. First, we are to teach our children that whatever gifts and skills they have are God-given and "are to be used in God's service." Secondly, we should help them discover what their gifts are. And thirdly, we should help them develop their gifts.

How Do We Help Our Children Discover Their Gifts?

Our children's behavior, thought processes, conversations, and interests will give us clues as to their spiritual gifts. These gifts often begin to emerge during the course of daily life. In the following paragraphs I am going to acquaint you with my children and their gifts. I hope doing this will provide you with some ideas and insights as you study your own children. Recognizing your children's spiritual gifts is not difficult if you make it a point to look for them. The home is the perfect place for your children to discover and begin to develop their gifts.

From the time my son Ty was six, I began noticing he had a true gift for evangelism. On one occasion, he was in the front yard playing with John. When I called the boys to come in to resume their schoolwork, Ty didn't come. I scolded him and told him that I expected him to obey me when I called him. I'll never forget his reply: "Mom, did you see that little boy? I was telling him about Jesus, and he seemed very interested. I thought I should finish talking to him before I came inside."

On another occasion, Joe had to go back to the office after dinner one night to complete a project he was working on. He decided to take Ty, who was eight, with him. On the way out of the office that night, Ty slipped his hand out of Joe's and walked back toward the security guard who had just let them out of the building. "Excuse me, Sir," Ty said, "are you a Christian?"

The man replied, "I go to church."

Ty responded politely, "But I asked if you are a Christian. Do you know Jesus?"

Joe ran into that security guard several weeks later. He told Joe that his encounter with Ty had changed his life. He was so touched by Ty's concern for him that this had led him to a renewed relationship with Christ.

On many more occasions, too numerous to mention here, Ty has talked to people powerfully about trusting in Jesus. The gift of evangelism fits Ty's personality. Ty is extremely outgoing, loves people, and loves to talk to them. It seems natural that he would talk to them about the most important thing in his life.

Ty is also tenderhearted and compassionate. As I review the lists in the preceding verses, I know that Ty's gifts include mercy, service, and generosity. Again, he has exhibited these traits since he was a little boy. Interestingly enough, I started noticing many of these positive characteristics when I took Ty out of kindergarten and began homeschooling him. We were free to emphasize the importance of service during the course of our homeschooling years, and this gave Ty the opportunity to develop his gifts of mercy, service, and generosity. (We will discuss the importance of service in depth in chapter 6.)

My son John also began exhibiting his gifts from a very early age. By the time John was two, he knew every word to four stanzas of many of the great hymns of the faith. I had always sung hymns to John at bedtime, and he learned them quickly and took them to heart. I had a book that I used for Bible memory with the boys. John went through this program quickly and began learning verses easily at the age of two. John has always been a deep thinker with an unusual ability to apply the knowledge he has obtained.

When my sister took Ty and John for a hike at Stone Mountain
State Park in Atlanta, Ty stopped John and exclaimed, "John, look
at this huge footprint. It's so big it must be God's!"

John, who was four at the time, quickly responded, "Ty, God is
a spirit and hath not a body like man."

John's gifts are born out of his deep understanding of theological issues and his desire to learn and grow and apply what he knows.
John also has always had an extremely sensitive conscience. As he
grew older, I affectionately referred to him as the Holy Spirit in our
house. He kept everyone walking the straight and narrow. John's
gifts are teaching, discernment, exhortation, and leading. As he has
gotten older, he has exhibited a real heart for evangelism as well.

Lizzy has always been discerning and adventurous. She is also
very talented in many facets of the performing arts, which can sometimes be a difficult arena for Christians. I have been her constant
companion as she has been involved in community theatre and other
pursuits. She has always amazed me at her ability to analyze almost
every situation from a scriptural perspective. Lizzy's spiritual gifts
include discernment and faith.

As Joe and I have discussed our goals for our children from
their youngest ages, we have both agreed that our greatest desire
has been for them to know Christ and to walk with Him on a daily
basis. Homeschooling the children has given us the opportunity to
focus on their spiritual lives and gifts. We know, however, that salvation is a gift of God, not of works, so that no man can boast.

Some children come to saving faith in Christ at a very early age. Others take a more circuitous route. Only God can change a heart. He alone gives spiritual gifts. God has graciously allowed parents to be participants in the process of raising children for His glory. In our homes we have the privilege of introducing our children to Christ, sharing His Word with them, and watching as their gifts and faith grow and unfold. This is perhaps the greatest blessing of parenting.

UNDERSTANDING YOUR CHILD'S BASIC PERSONALITY

Personality is defined as "the complex of characteristics that distinguishes a particular individual or individualizes or characterizes him in his relationships with others."[13] Gaining a basic understanding of your child's personality is crucial as you work with him to help him discern his bent—how God has created him. Developing insight into each child's personality also contributes to family harmony and unity.

The diversity of personalities we have in our home never ceases to amaze me. How could our three children be so different? I know families with eight and ten children who express the same sentiment. Personalities materialize almost as quickly as children emerge from the womb. Some children are compliant from birth. Others enter the world announcing that they intend to be in charge. Some children are task oriented, while others are people oriented.

Understanding your child's personality takes on new significance if you and your child have different personalities. You might
be surprised and somewhat annoyed to learn that your child does not
react to problems or conflict in the way that you do.

My husband and I have found two tools over the years that have
helped us as we have tried to understand and work with each child's
personality and bent. The first is a personality survey tool developed
by John Trent and Gary Smalley that groups personalities into four
categories: lion, otter, golden retriever, and beaver.[14] We watched a
video series on this topic when our children were younger because we
really wanted to understand what motivated and inspired each of
them.

Here is a sample of some of the characteristics of each personality type:

The lion: "takes charge, determined, assertive, firm,
enterprising, competitive, enjoys challenges, bold, purposeful, decision maker, leader, goal-driven, self-reliant,
adventurous."[15]

The otter: "takes risks, visionary, motivator, energetic,
very verbal, promoter, avoids details, fun-loving, likes
variety, enjoys change, creative, group-oriented, mixes
easily, optimistic."[16]

The golden retriever: "loyal, nondemanding, even keel,
avoids conflict, enjoys routine, dislikes change, deep relationships, adaptable, sympathetic, thoughtful, nurturing,
patient, tolerant, good listener."[17]

The beaver: "deliberate, controlled, reserved, predictable, practical, orderly, factual, discerning, detailed, analytical, inquisitive, precise, persistent, scheduled."[18]

Focus on the Family's *Parents' Guide to the Spiritual Growth of Children* by John Trent, Rick Osborne, and Kurt Bruner devotes a chapter to helping parents diagnose their children's personality types and also helps parents understand how to encourage, motivate, and teach each personality type.[19] You can also order and take personality surveys online using the lion, otter, golden retriever, and beaver model through Ministry Insights at www.ministryinsights.com.

My oldest son, Ty (who is now twenty-seven), is a total otter—an energetic, extroverted, people-person. I attended a banquet last week that he helped organize. An elderly man, whom I did not know, approached me and gave me a big hug. "Are you Ty's mom?" he asked. When I replied that I was, he told me how surprised he was that I didn't look old and haggard. When I gave him a puzzled look, he continued on, "I love Ty. He is fun, energetic, thoughtful, and he gets things done. But, Mrs. Tyler, I have only known Ty for three weeks, and he has already worn me out. I can't imagine being his mother!"

Ty's personality, in many ways, defined our early years of homeschooling. Because John is caring and unselfish (the survey would say because he is part golden retriever), he felt the need to help take care of Ty, even though Ty is two years older. John flexed a lot for Ty's sake. While John preferred structure, he was willing to be spontaneous for Ty. When Lizzy came along, I finally realized that she did not enjoy spontaneous assignments or field trips. She needed plenty of warning to plan her schedule and get her ducks in a row.

While overcategorizing people is not a good habit to develop, these designations are helpful in understanding why members in the same family often react differently to the same situations and events. This information also enables you to anticipate and prepare for the way your children might respond to difficult circumstances and people in their lives. Knowledge of each child's personality will help you plan more effectively as you endeavor to help your child succeed in life. If you can help him understand his strengths and his weaknesses, and why he reacts the way he does, your child will be well equipped to tackle the race that has been set before him.

The second personality assessment tool Joe and I used in our home is the DISC™. According to their Web site, DISC is the "original, oldest, most validated, reliable, personal assessment used by over 50 million others to improve lives, relationships, work productivity, teamwork, teams, and communication."[20] DISC divides personality types into four primary categories: Dominance (D); Influence (I), Steadiness (S), and Conscientiousness (C). These categories correspond somewhat to the lion, otter, golden retriever, and beaver. The DISC tests are available online (www.Disc Profile.com) or in a paper format.

Recently, while speaking at Sally Clarkson's WholeHeart Mother Conference in Dallas, I shared this information on personality styles. At the conclusion of my workshop, a mother gave me a copy of a book entitled *Praying for Your Child (According to His or Her*

Personality Style) by Beth McLendon and Robert A. Rohn, Ph.D.
This book not only describes each personality type, but gives discipline tips for each type. The prayer guide is an added bonus, giving
focus to our parental prayers on behalf of our children. You can also
order their personality test (based on the DISC model) online at
www.personalityinsight.com. You or your child can take the appropriate version online, and then have the results E-mailed to you.

Studying your child's personality, whether you decide to use one
of these particular assessment tools or not, plays an important role in
helping your child discover his bent. Personality and spiritual gifts
are often closely tied, though not always. Understanding personality
is an important step in helping your children understand and discern
their purpose in life.

Determining Your Child's Learning Style(s)

When I began homeschooling in 1984, I had never heard of
learning styles. Ty was six, and I was using a curriculum that was
totally unsuited for him, but I was bound by an archaic homeschooling law that required me to use the same curriculum as a public or private school in our district. Every morning, according to our
curriculum, I was to begin teaching by saying something along these
lines: (This is a loose paraphrase because I have long since pitched
that curriculum.) "Children, sit up straight in your chairs with your
feet on the floor and your hands folded and placed on your desks. Be
sure to look me in the eye when I am talking to you."

At age six, Ty could not sit still to save his life. Some part of him was always moving. Most days his wiggling and squirming did not bother me. But one day I awoke with a new resolve. I decided I had been too easy on Ty, and I needed to be tougher. "Today," I thought, "will be the day Ty sits still and straight, with his feet and hands properly situated, while looking me in the eye while I teach him."

Well, as you can imagine, the day was disastrous. Ty did sit still for a couple of hours, but he was totally miserable, and so was I. The thing that amazed me the most was how little he seemed to understand from our school work that day. Ty always interacted with me about what we were studying, and he could almost always answer questions about the material we were studying. Not this day. He sat still, to be sure, but he learned nothing.

I quickly abandoned my new drill-sergeant resolve, and we continued with our more pleasant version of homeschooling. I still continued to entertain nagging thoughts that I was not being strict enough with Ty; but although I could not explain it, the more he talked and moved, the more he seemed to learn. The stiller he sat, the less he learned.

One day, Ty, John, and I visited our favorite toy store to buy a birthday present for one of their friends. This toy store had a book rack that I always gravitated towards while the boys played with the wooden Brio train set that I could never afford to buy them. This particular day, I picked up a book entitled *Growing Up Learning: The Key to Your Child's Potential*[21] by Walter B. Barbe, Ph.D. As I read through the book's foreword, examined the table of contents, and breezed through the body of the book, I felt as if someone had placed pure gold in my hands.

I quickly bought the book and birthday present, gathered up the boys, and headed home. I read the rest of the day. I couldn't put the book down. Dr. Barbe provided me with the information I needed to learn how to effectively teach Ty—and eventually all of my children. His work at the time (1985) was groundbreaking.

Dr. Barbe sets the stage for the rest of his book in the introduction, entitled "The Key to Your Child's Potential."

> We each learn in our own special way. How we learn is determined by what we are born with and by our experiences in life. Many factors, therefore, can influence the way we learn best. Perception is the way we gain meaning from sensations. While we perceive through all our senses, in most learning situations the most relevant are sight, hearing, and kinesthesia (touch and movement).
>
> My research and that of many other educational psychologists indicate that each of us relies predominantly on one of these three, our strongest, when we are mastering a new skill or concept. We call this our *learning strength* or *modality strength.*[22]

Dr. Barbe defines the three modalities as visual, auditory, and kinesthetic. He then provides chapters on how to identify your learning strength as a parent and how to identify your child's learning strength. I discovered that I am a visual/auditory learner while Ty is an auditory/kinesthetic learner. He learns by talking and doing.

With every page I read I felt as if lights were flashing and bells were ringing. "If the kinesthetic child can survive school, he can do very well in life."[23] "In a classroom situation demanding quiet and stillness, the auditory/kinesthetic child is always at a disadvantage. She is rarely allowed to use her strengths. The very thing she wants to do to get involved in learning are the things that get her into trouble."[24]

And, finally, came the answer I had been looking for as to why Ty had seemed to learn nothing the day I insisted that he sit perfectly still. Dr Barbe revealed the answer as he discussed another person's problem. "After hearing about modality, she now understood that she was kinesthetic, not visual. She had spent her energy controlling her need for physical movement. She had barely made it through school; she had not, and still did not, enjoy learning. The effort it took her to sit still did not allow her to learn as well as she could have."[25]

Eureka! I found it! That day God placed information in my hands and in my heart that changed our family's life forever. I felt free for the first time to let Ty be Ty, rather than always feeling the need to insist that he be still and quiet. In retrospect, discovering learning modalities, learning strengths, and learning styles reminded me of watching Shane fold those twenty-three maps after my co-op class. I felt like I could finally work with Ty's bent, rather than fighting against it. This information set Ty free to be and to learn how God had designed him.

Cathy Duffy provides an excellent explanation and presentation of learning modalities and learning styles in chapter 4 of her new book *100 Top Picks for Homeschool Curriculum*: "The term *learning style* refers to the way (or style) a person most easily learns and processes new information or skills. Learning styles are just a bit more complex than learning modalities. Learning styles include awareness of children's preferred learning modalities, but they go further to look at other personality/learning traits, such as a desire to work with other people or independently, an orientation toward either the big picture or the details, and preferences for a more- or less-structured environment."[26]

After Cathy thoroughly explains the importance of learning styles and the different theories and approaches that are being used today, she helps parents diagnose their own learning styles and then helps them diagnose each of their children's learning styles. I cannot recommend Cathy's treatment of this subject highly enough. The information is current, easily discernible, and will make a difference in how you teach and view your children.[27]

As the information explosion continues, the process of learning becomes a key component of the educational equation. If we can instill in our children a love for learning, they will be lifelong learners. If they master the process of learning, they can become independent learners and thinkers who know how and where to find the information they need in an age where information is vitally important, but the sheer volume of it makes it impossible to master.

Helping our children decipher how they learn the most effectively and efficiently is an invaluable gift in today's world. This is an important part of helping them discover their bent and their unique purpose in life.

DISCOVERING YOUR CHILD'S STRENGTHS

This entire chapter has, in a sense, been devoted to helping you find your child's areas of strength. We learned first that all children are strengthened as they are loved unconditionally. As we moved into discussions of spiritual gifts, personality traits, and learning styles, we examined ways to determine your child's areas of giftedness. These areas of giftedness make up a substantial portion of your child's overall strengths.

We would be abandoning this discourse on discovering strengths prematurely if we failed to discuss how our children need to use these strengths.

Dr. Barbe sheds important light on this subject in the following paragraphs:

> As an adult, you have most likely learned through experience to transfer information from one channel to another, and to apply your learning strength in areas that are difficult. One of the sure signs of being an adult is knowing just what you are weak in. No one will ever catch us doing something willingly, especially in front of others, that we know we don't do well.

Our children are not so lucky. In many academic settings, they are tested and confronted with their failures. They are given endless hours of practice, not in their areas of strength, but in their areas of weakness. Eventually this can destroy their self-confidence and their willingness to learn. At home, too, we expect our children to do things the way we do. If our learning strength is different from theirs, we may not be reinforcing their strengths.[28]

First, we must teach our children what it means to operate from their strengths. While this seems obvious and elementary to us, we need to verbalize this principle to our children. Discuss your child's spiritual gifts with him, and how God gave him particular gifts to benefit the church. Discuss your child's personality type with him, and explain the strengths and weaknesses associated with it. Help your child discern how he learns best, and make sure he understands how to approach academics in a way that draws from his area of strength. Depending on the ages of your children, they might not understand all that you are trying to relate to them, but as they grow up with this type of conversation in the home, they will be particularly well-equipped to take their God-given places in this world.

Before we leave this discussion on strengths, we should address actual talents and skills your children currently possess or will develop based on their particular bent, their gifts, their interests, and their strengths. Because you have carefully cultivated your child's underground root system, one day the seed that has been growing will erupt through the ground's surface and begin to bear fruit upward. Remember Isaiah 37:31? "The surviving remnant of the house of Judah will again take root downward and bear fruit upward."

This fruit will manifest itself in a number of different ways, in different spheres, and at different times in your child's life. I often think of Eric Liddle's love for running. Liddle, a Scotsman, was preparing to go to China as a missionary when he competed in the 1924 Olympic Games. Even though Liddle refused to run in his best event because it was held on Sunday, he went on to set a world record in the 400 meters. He won a gold medal in this event, although many had questioned whether he would even be able to place in it. The 1981 movie *Chariots of Fire* made Liddle a hero and a role model for Christian athletes everywhere. In this movie, Eric Liddle makes the following statement to his sister: "I know that God has made me for a purpose, to be a missionary in China. But he also made me fast. And when I run, I feel His pleasure."

We should always be watching our children to identify their true passions. These will be the areas in their lives where, like Eric Liddle, they can feel God's pleasure. These passions may be vocations or avocations. It doesn't matter. Whatever they are, like Liddle, God can use our children's gifts and abilities to display His glory to a watching world.

Conclusion

Isaac Watts, the great hymn writer, penned the words to the hymn "Jesus Shall Reign Where'er the Sun" in 1719.[29] In the fifth verse, which is often hard to find, Watts proclaims, "Let every creature rise and bring peculiar honors to our King." Watts helps us in the task of keeping an eternal perspective by eloquently articulating our ultimate goal as Christian parents: we are to aid our children in the process of cultivating their potential in every area of life. We are to help them discover their unique gifts and calling in this life so that one day they will be able to "rise and bring" their peculiar (unique, particular) honors to our King.

chapter five

TOOL NUMBER 4

developing worldview

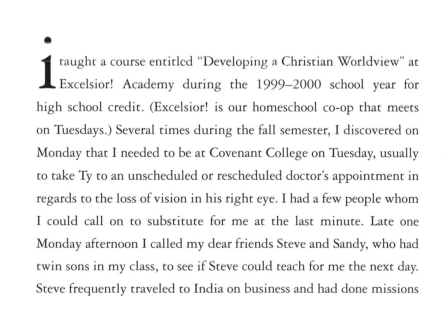

i taught a course entitled "Developing a Christian Worldview" at
Excelsior! Academy during the 1999–2000 school year for
high school credit. (Excelsior! is our homeschool co-op that meets
on Tuesdays.) Several times during the fall semester, I discovered on
Monday that I needed to be at Covenant College on Tuesday, usually
to take Ty to an unscheduled or rescheduled doctor's appointment in
regards to the loss of vision in his right eye. I had a few people whom
I could call on to substitute for me at the last minute. Late one
Monday afternoon I called my dear friends Steve and Sandy, who had
twin sons in my class, to see if Steve could teach for me the next day.
Steve frequently traveled to India on business and had done missions

work while he was there. I knew the students in my class would benefit greatly from hearing how a successful businessman had powerfully and effectively incorporated his faith into his profession. Steve graciously agreed to teach for me.

When I returned from Tennessee, I called Sandy and Steve to ask about the class. Sandy answered the phone and greeted my question with laughter. "When you called on Monday, Steve quickly agreed to teach your worldview class. Right after agreeing to do that, he looked at me and said, 'What's worldview?'"

What Is Worldview?

Steve is not alone in asking that question. Many of us grew up in a world where God was welcome. We lived in two-parent families and went to church regularly. Devotions were even part of the daily routine of the elementary school I attended. Everyone seemed to share a similar worldview. In the sixties and seventies, however, the country began exiting en masse from these traditional values of faith and family.

By the time I reached high school, the attitude toward God was decidedly different from those early elementary years. As a junior in high school, I gave the invocation at one of our high school football games. My high school had close to three thousand students, and we always had big crowds at the games. I don't remember exactly what I said in that prayer. I do know that I spoke of Jesus and prayed in His name. The next day I was called to the principal's office and asked to apologize to a community leader and a student I had offended. I did say that I was sorry I had offended them, but I could not apologize for saying the name of Jesus in public. Times were changing.

Dr. J. Budziszewski, associate professor of government and philosophy at the University of Texas in Austin, made this observation several years ago about our current American culture.

> We Christians are now outnumbered by people who do not share our presuppositions, and for the first time in American history, the word of God is unwelcome out of church. This is a new situation for Christians in our country. We have never known a civic rhetoric that was not based on the Bible. The Scriptures were the foundation of American public speech from the colonies onward, not only among believers, but even among nonbelievers. Historians still argue about whether President Abraham Lincoln was a Christian. Yet he talked like one. His Second Inaugural Address—perhaps the greatest American speech ever delivered—is little more than an application of the Nineteenth Psalm to the dreadful War Between the States. Moreover, when Lincoln said, "the judgments of the Lord are true and righteous altogether," he could be sure that almost all of his fellow citizens would recognize the allusion and feel its force, irrespective of their particular religious affiliation.[1]

America has gone from a country that once welcomed God (and His Word) to one where His Word is unwelcome outside the church. When a Christian view of the world prevailed in our society, being able to define *worldview* was not so important. Now that we live in a society that prefers to view the world apart from God, Christians must educate themselves on what a biblical worldview is and why it's important. As Christian parents, we must commit ourselves to understanding worldview issues for our children's sake because they are confronted daily with peer pressure and a pop culture that are often openly hostile to their values. If we choose to remain ignorant, our children's faith will suffer.

Author, attorney, and radio commentator Chuck Colson defines *worldview* as "simply the sum total of our beliefs about the world, the 'big picture' that directs our daily decisions and actions."[2]

In *Thinking Like A Christian: Understanding and Living a Biblical Worldview,* Dr. David Noebel further develops the concept of worldview: "The term 'worldview' refers to any ideology, philosophy, theology, movement, or religion that provides an overarching approach to understanding God, the world, and man's relationship to the world. Specifically, a worldview should provide a particular perspective on each of the following ten disciplines: theology, philosophy, biology, psychology, ethics, sociology, law, politics, economics, and history. These disciplines also have implications for cultural expression such as found in the visual and performing arts, music, and literature. Since biblical Christianity offers a specific stance or attitude toward all ten disciplines, it is, by our definition, a worldview."[3]

As Christian parents, we must boldly transmit a consistent, biblical worldview to our children for two reasons: worldview will give both *focus* and *direction* to our children's lives.

WORLDVIEW BRINGS FOCUS

My entire fourth-grade class was called to the school cafeteria one day for routine vision screenings. When my turn came, the school nurse asked me to identify which way the Es were pointing on the 20/20 line of the eye chart. "What Es?" I asked. I could see none. Actually, I could not see anything on the eye chart at all that day, except for the very large E at the top. The school nurse, visibly upset by my lack of vision, exclaimed, "Honey, you're almost blind!"

In tears, I tore out of the cafeteria and ran straight for my mother's classroom. I burst into her room unannounced and hysterically repeated the school nurse's prognostication—I was going blind. My mother and I left school that day and went straight to see the ophthalmologist. He confirmed that my vision had certainly deteriorated—I was extremely nearsighted with a severe astigmatism—but he also assured us that I was not going blind.

Two weeks later I picked up my first pair of glasses. I put them on and was astounded at what I could see. It was the Christmas holidays, and that same day we visited a large toy store to do some shopping. I could see toys at the end of the aisles. I could see the faces of the people pushing shopping carts. I remember thinking, *I can see everything, and it is all so clear.* I kept taking my glasses off and putting them back on, amazed each time at how this little pair of glasses (with very thick lenses) brought the whole world into focus for me.

A biblical worldview is like those glasses—it brings the whole world into focus. When we teach our children to view all of life through the lens of Scripture, we are giving them a priceless gift in today's secular society.

WORLDVIEW GIVES DIRECTION IN LIFE

As I mentioned in an earlier chapter, Lizzy served as a news reporter intern for WMHK, a Christian radio station, during her junior year of high school. One concern Joe and I had about her taking the intern position at WMHK was her inability to find her way around Columbia and the outlying areas. She had not been driving long, and Lizzy, like her mother, is directionally challenged.

One of her first assignments from Bob Holmes, the news director, was to cover a press conference at the State House. Lizzy, at age sixteen, was not at all concerned or intimidated by covering a press conference convened and attended by state senators. She grew up in that environment because we have worked on homeschooling legislation as a family her entire life. Her only concern was getting there. Lizzy was relieved to learn that she was making this first trip with Mr. Holmes, and she planned to pay careful attention to the route he chose to get to the State House from the radio station, knowing that she would make that trip many times during the course of the year.

Lizzy called me the morning of the press conference, whispering from a back line in the studio that Mr. Holmes couldn't go after all; she was left to drive to the capitol by herself.

I had instructed Lizzy not to drive and talk on her cell phone simultaneously. "Today," I explained to her on the phone, "is an exception." I talked Lizzy all the way to the State House, giving her landmarks, interstate exits, and street names to watch for. Our conversation did not end until I had her parked and headed in the right direction. Or so I thought.

Lizzy called me back a few minutes later to tell me she had evidently taken a wrong turn while walking to the State House and was standing in front of the State Department of Education instead. As I puzzled over how to get her to the right place, I had a sudden inspiration.

"Lizzy, turn around and look up. Do you see the dome?"

"Yes, ma'am."

"That's the State House dome. Walk toward the dome. As long as it is getting bigger, you are going in the right direction. Keep your eyes on the dome."

Lizzy called a few minutes later to say she was inside the State House with her equipment set up.

A biblical worldview, like the State House dome, serves as a compass for our children, giving them a point of reference that is steady and reliable. It gives the landmark they need to find their way in this world and to help them stay the course.

When Faith and Worldview Collide

Worldview is not something we learn about so we can take pride in what we know. Neither is worldview static and stale. A Christian worldview is empowering and ennobling because God and His Word are at the center of it. When we come face-to-face with the claims of Christ and acknowledge Him as Lord, His Spirit replaces our view of the world with His. The apostle Paul is a good example. Before his Damascus Road conversion, Paul energetically embraced the worldview of a Pharisee. He was actively and proudly persecuting Christians. When God knocked Paul down and confronted him on the road to Damascus, Paul's worldview changed in an instant.

In chapter 3, on cultivating intimacy, we talked about the power of God's presence in our lives. Not only is God's presence active and powerful, but so is His Word: "For the word of God is living and effective and sharper than any two-edged sword, penetrating as far as to divide soul, spirit, joints, and marrow; it is a judge of the ideas and thoughts of the heart" (Heb. 4:12).

Martin Luther recognized the power of the Word of God. He said, "I opposed Indulgences . . . but never with force. I simply taught, preached, and wrote God's Word; otherwise I did nothing."[4] Luther went on to say that while he slept and fellowshipped with his friends, the power of the Word worked in the world. "I did nothing; the Word did everything."[5] Luther's life had been transformed by faith in Christ and the Word of God. Luther did not keep this transformation to himself. His goal was not to change the world. It certainly wasn't to start the Protestant Reformation. As Luther committed his life to God and His view of the world, God worked powerfully through Luther to impact the world. God will do the same with us and our children. If we will offer Him what we have, our five loaves and two fish, He will take our meager resources and use them mightily in this world. This is the life of faith.

Hebrews 11, the faith chapter, defines much of what a biblical worldview involves. Interestingly enough, the first evidence of faith mentioned in the chapter is a belief in creation: "By faith we understand that the universe was created by the word of God, so that what is seen has been made from things that are not visible" (v. 3). Creation is one bedrock of the biblical worldview. "In the beginning God created the heavens and the earth."

A biblical worldview always seeks to combine the Word of God with faith. Hebrews 11 is full of stories of the lives of ordinary men and women who transformed their world because of their faith in God. Hebrews 11 tells of Abel, Enoch, Noah, Abraham, Sarah, Isaac, Joseph, and Moses and his parents, for starters. Then we learn of more: "For time will fail me if I tell of Gideon, Barak, Samson, Jephthah, of David and Samuel and the prophets, who by faith conquered kingdoms, performed acts of righteousness, obtained promises, shut the mouths of lions, quenched the power of fire, escaped the edge of the sword, from weakness were made strong, became mighty in war, put foreign armies to flight" (Heb. 11:32–34 NASB). Tell these stories to your children often so these stories of faith become their own.

Martin Luther's insight about the work of the Word of God in the world should encourage us greatly as parents. Martin Luther trusted God to do great things in the world that he knew he (Luther) couldn't do. As parents, we can do the same. We can trust God to work powerfully in our children's lives through His Word and through His Spirit, even when our knowledge and resources are inadequate.

Three Obstacles to Developing Christian Worldview

A strong biblical worldview constantly seeks ways to integrate all areas of our lives under the direction and the power of the Word of God. Some of the main obstacles that can stifle worldview growth and development in us and our children have to do with separating things that were never meant to be separated.

OBSTACLE 1—THE SEPARATION OF SACRED AND SECULAR

Many modern Christians have a bad habit of compartmentalizing their spiritual lives. Going to church on Sunday has nothing to do with life on Monday through Saturday. While church attendance is part of the culture, it is an activity that will never affect their lives. In this scenario, the secular rules while the sacred is given lip service.

The opposite scenario also plagues modern Christians. We think that spirituality is defined *only* by reading the Bible, prayer, fellowship, and other spiritual pursuits. Charles Colson takes issue with this:

> But if we are to restore our world, we first have to shake off the comfortable notion that Christianity is merely a personal experience, applying to one's private life.[6]
>
> Don't get me wrong. We need prayer, Bible study, worship, fellowship, and witnessing. But if we focus exclusively on these disciplines and if in the process we ignore our responsibility to redeem the surrounding culture—our Christianity will remain privatized and marginalized.[7]
>
> We must show the world that Christianity is more than private belief, more than personal salvation. We must show that it is a comprehensive life system that answers all of humanity's age-old questions: Where did I come from? Why am I here? Where am I going? Does life have meaning and purpose?[8]

One of the greatest dichotomies that has plagued the church historically is the idea of "sacred calling" versus "secular calling." The early church often viewed work as "a debasing and demeaning activity, best left to one's social—and spiritual—inferiors."[9] People who worked for a living were viewed by many in the early church and the monastic movement as second-class Christians. Only "full-time" Christian work was deemed truly spiritual.[10]

The leaders of the sixteenth-century Reformation energetically refuted this claim. Beginning with Martin Luther and continuing with John Calvin, they developed an idea of calling and vocation that we now refer to as the Protestant work ethic.[11] This principle sees all work as valuable and infused with meaning when it is done for the glory of God. "Luther totally rejected the notion that monks and clergy were engaged in holier work than shopkeepers and housewives. 'Seemingly secular works are a worship of God,' he wrote, 'and an obedience well pleasing to God.'"[12]

As is often the case, we too quickly forget some of history's most valuable lessons. By the mid-1900s, acclaimed British author and essayist Dorothy Sayers felt compelled to pen these words: "In nothing has the Church so lost Her hold on reality as in Her failure to understand and respect the secular vocation. She has allowed work and religion to become separate departments. . . . She has forgotten that the secular vocation is sacred. . . . How can anyone remain interested in a religion which seems to have no concern with nine-tenths of his life?"[13]

You may be asking yourself, "What in the world does this have to do with cultivating my child's potential?"

The Southern Baptist Council on Family Life conducted some compelling research in 2002 that revealed that 88 percent of children raised in evangelical homes leave the church when they turn eighteen. They never return.[14] Eighty-eight percent! That is catastrophic. Research by George Barna and others substantiates these findings.[15]

Many children lose interest in Christianity because they do not understand its implications for their daily lives. As parents, we must continually demonstrate to our children that Christianity is relevant to all of life and that God is intimately interested in every aspect of their lives—including their hobbies and career interests, their work and their play, their strengths and their weaknesses. If we fail to do that, our children will become part of that 88 percent clamoring to run out the church door when they become "of age."

We must communicate to our children that each of them, in God's economy, brings important gifts to employ in this world for God's glory and our neighbor's welfare. That is why we work. The engineer, the doctor, the mother, the lawyer, the car mechanic, the writer all serve God by doing their work well—by using their gifts to solve problems and improve the world. This idea of improving the world at every level is what God told Adam and Eve to do in the Garden of Eden: He commanded them, through their work, to fill the earth and subdue it (to tame it, improve it, and increase its productivity).

Colson takes us back to the Genesis idea of "drawing out potential":

In the opening chapters of Genesis, we learn that human beings were made in the image of God, to reflect his character; therefore, we are called to reflect his creative activity through our own creativity—by cultivating the world, drawing out its potential, and giving it shape and form. All work has dignity as an expression of the divine image."[16]

We need to present this view of work and the world to our children—this view that refuses to separate the sacred from the secular. If we can help them to understand that every aspect of life is sacred as we offer it to God, than we are giving them a vision that is invigorating and sustaining. We all want our children to be in that small minority that continues following Christ beyond adolescence.

OBSTACLE 2—THE SEPARATION OF CHURCH AND SOCIETY

The separation of church and state gets a lot of play in the media today, mainly because of groups like the ACLU (the American Civil Liberties Union). The goal is to make sure every vestige of Christianity is wiped clean from the public square—from politics and government, from education, and from the legal system—even from the Pledge of Allegiance! The ultimate goal is to become a society that forgets God. We discussed the consequences of forgetting God as a society in chapter 2—everything becomes random and purposeless.

Part of your job in helping your children develop a biblical worldview is to call these things (like the purging of God from society) to your children's attention and discuss them. Do not let your children forget God. Become well-versed enough in these issues to talk about them with your children. (If you need help in knowing how to do this, see "Available Resources" toward the end of this chapter.) Remember that God Himself encourages us to talk constantly to our children about God and the meaning of life: "These words that I am giving you today are to be in your heart. Repeat them to your children. Talk about them when you sit in your house and when you walk along the road, when you lie down and when you get up" (Deut. 6:6–7). God ordained conversation to be a powerful tool for us as parents to use in equipping our children with a biblical worldview.

Dr. David Noebel, college professor, author, and founder of Summit Ministries, has this to say about current trends in Western civilization and the separation of the church from society:

> The biblical worldview was the nursery of Western civilization and the foundation of the American experiment in ordered liberty. Yet today, Christianity is in retreat in almost every area of our society. This retreat began over 150 years ago when the great revivals that swept the country focused on the emotions and not the mind. Later in the early 1900s, the church found itself unprepared to face the intellectual challenges of liberal theology and withdrew further into its shell, shielding itself from *the primary shapers of culture—education, politics, and the media.* The void left by a lack of Christian influence has been predictable—an increasingly dark and tasteless society.[17] (author emphasis)

The Three Culture Shapers: Politics, The Media, and Education

The 2004 presidential election was a watershed event in our society and may very well signal a turning of the tide. The electorate rose up and declared that moral issues are important to a majority of Americans. President George W. Bush, a self-proclaimed Christian, defeated liberal Senator John Kerry. Same-sex marriage initiatives were defeated in every state that offered them on the ballot. Even during a time of war and a somewhat ailing economy, American Christians have impacted the culture in a significant way by voting their conscience in a troubled world. Christians may once again be effective in politics—one of the shapers of culture.

Make sure you are keeping your children in the political loop. Find candidates who share your values and beliefs and work in these campaigns together. Visit your state legislator or senator together. Take your children with you to vote. As you are involved in the world, make sure to include your children in your activities. There is no better way to teach them how to be positively involved in your church and community than to lead by example. (We will discuss specific civics and political activities and programs in chapter 8.)

Christians are even making some inroads in the media—another culture shaper. Conservative commentators who exhibit an understanding of biblical moral and family values are becoming more and more popular on both television and radio. On the print side, *WORLD* magazine reports the news from a Christian worldview perspective. The Internet has provided a forum for Christians to communicate in a variety of ways. Many Christian organizations have e-newsletters that are great sources of information about the work of the church and Christian organizations in the world. Chuck Colson's *Breakpoint,* a daily radio program and e-newsletter, gives a solid Christian worldview perspective on

world events. That newsletter alone provides quality information that
you can read with your children and discuss on a daily basis. Use a
combination of these media resources as a springboard for discussion
as you teach your children about current events from a biblical perspective. Their understanding of our society will grow, while the
temptation to withdraw from it will diminish.

In giving your children an understanding of the importance of the
media in society, coupled with the ability to filter what they see and
hear through the lens of Scripture, you are strengthening their worldview and reinforcing the important role Christians play in shaping the
culture. As your children get older, your efforts will help them stay con-
nected to the church, and hopefully their efforts will help the church
continue to impact the world rather than withdraw from the world.

The first shaper of culture that Noebel mentioned, and the last
one that we will discuss here, is education. Nowhere have more
ardent efforts been made to purge our society of Christianity than in
the public school system. The judicial system and social activists
have aimed their combined fire-power at the public schools of the
land to make sure every mention of God is eradicated. As long ago
as 1837, Horace Mann, often referred to "as the father of public
education," made this statement: "What the church has been for
medieval man, the public school must become for democratic and
rational man. God will be replaced by the concept of the public
good. . . . The common [public] schools . . . shall create a more far-
seeing intelligence and a more pure morality than has ever existed
among communities of men."[18]

Christian parents, in record numbers, are beginning to seek educational alternatives where they have the freedom to teach their children from a biblical perspective. Many parents are choosing to homeschool; the number of homeschooled students is growing exponentially. At the time of this writing, there are more than two million homeschooled students in the United States. Homeschoolers are distinguishing themselves academically—scoring higher than their traditionally-schooled counterparts on the SAT and ACT (tests used for college admissions). Homeschooled students, on average, are scoring between the 70th and 85th percentile on nationally-normed standardized tests; the average score for public school students is the 50th percentile. Homeschoolers are also routinely winning a variety of academic competitions like geography and spelling bees.

While these successes are exciting, I believe the greatest story of the homeschooling movement is yet to be told. Homeschooled children are not growing up to be social misfits as many have feared; as a matter of fact, the opposite is true. Homeschooled students are demonstrating leadership skills that are every bit as exceptional as their academic achievements. Additionally, Christian homeschooling actively promotes and encourages faith and the development of a strong, vibrant biblical worldview. I believe that these children—who have been raised in homes that are committed to establishing identity and cultivating intimacy, where individual abilities and strong biblical worldviews are nurtured—will have the gifts and the motivation necessary to make significant contributions to the world. Their faith in God will be their biggest asset, empowering them and informing them as they strive to

lead productive lives of service, work, and worship. They will contribute to society, not separate from it or abandon it.

For more information on facts and statistics concerning the success of homeschool students, I would recommend the *2005–2006
Worldwide Guide to Homeschooling: Facts and Stats on the Benefits of
Homeschooling.* The author, Dr. Brian Ray, is the president of the
National Home Education Research Institute and the homeschooling father of eight children. This version includes Dr. Ray's
latest research on the success of homeschooled graduates. Whether
you are a parent, journalist, policy maker, professional educator,
researcher, or curious grandparent, this book will help you understand homeschoolers and the homeschool movement.[19]

OBSTACLE 3—THE SEPARATION OF CHRISTIANITY AND THE MIND

In an article entitled "Overcoming the Scandal of the Christian
Mind," Dr. Budziszewski writes the following: "In 1993, when
Washington Post writer Michael Weisskopf issued his notorious declaration that evangelicals are 'largely poor, uneducated, and easy to
command,' conservative Protestant intellectuals were quick to call
his bluff. Yet only a year later, when historian Mark Noll, himself a
conservative Protestant, published a book called *The Scandal of the
Evangelical Mind,* it was widely greeted by his coreligionists not with
cries of 'Scoundrel!' and 'Traitor!' but the murmur, 'Alas, 'tis true.' "[20]

During the course of the article, Dr. Budziszewski makes the
point that evangelicals really aren't backward or stupid, but we have

focused on God's "special revelation" (the Bible) to the exclusion of His "general revelation" (the world around us). In other words, we have separated the sacred and the secular, failing to develop a comprehensive, compelling biblical worldview equipped to explain both the complexities and intricacies of life. He concludes this point with a glimpse into his life as a college professor:

> Perhaps I am sensitive to the problem because I spend time around college students, who are a cultural magnifying glass. Surrounded by neopagans, young evangelicals have no idea how to translate biblical concepts into language that friends and hostile teachers can understand. Worse, there are whole continents of life in which their faith does not function at all. The cables just haven't been connected. A bright, Bible-minded student may be able to discourse learnedly about what Paul said to the Ephesians, but if you ask him to explain what the triune God has to do with his intended profession of biochemistry, engineering, or commercial law, he comes to a dead stop. None of those things are in his Bible's concordance.[21]

It hasn't always been this way. Many of America's founders were committed Christians and brilliant thinkers, whose contributions to the world were powerful and significant. The Pilgrims were able to synthesize all they knew of Scripture and governance, and write the Mayflower Compact, the first document of its kind in the history of the world to establish self-government.[22]

John Winthrop was a successful lawyer, as well as the founder and the first governor of the Massachusetts Bay Colony (re-elected eleven consecutive times). He said, "We shall find that the God of Israel is among us, when ten of us shall be able to resist a thousand of our enemies, when He shall make us a praise and glory, that men of succeeding plantations shall say, 'The Lord make it like that of New England.' For we must consider that we shall be as a City upon a Hill, the eyes of all people are upon us."[23]

Finally, the great orator and statesman Patrick Henry boldly stated, "It cannot be emphasized too strongly or too often that this great nation was founded, not by religionists, but by Christians; not on religions, but on the Gospel of Jesus Christ. For this very reason peoples of other faiths have been afforded asylum, prosperity, and freedom of worship here."[24]

Additionally, many of our greatest academic institutions were founded on Christian principles. Harvard's "Rules and Precepts," from the year 1646, included this statement: "Let every student be plainly instructed, and earnestly pressed to consider well, the main end of his life and studies is, to know God and Jesus Christ which is eternal life (John 17:3) and therefore lay Christ at the bottom, as the only foundation of all sound knowledge and learning."[25]

Remember that these examples and quotes are not given to convince you that America's heritage is strictly Christian. The Enlightenment created a number of Deists, including Thomas Jefferson. The point is to realize that Christianity has produced some of our country's greatest thinkers; there is no reason why this can't once again be true. Homeschooling again stands ready to fill in the gap. We have already established that homeschooled students are excelling academically. If they are raised with a biblical worldview that emphasizes integrating faith into all areas of life, they will be well-equipped to positively and significantly impact society.

Available Resources for Developing Worldview

After speaking at a state homeschooling convention on the topic of "Helping Children Develop a Christian Worldview," I had a distraught mother approach me. She said, "I didn't grow up in the church, and I attended public schools and a secular university. How am I going to train my children to have a biblical worldview if I don't know how to think that way myself?"

I sat down with her and together we went through material developed by Dr. David Noebel and Chuck Edwards designed to teach biblical worldview. There are actually two courses. The first is *Thinking Like a Christian: Understanding and Living a Biblical Worldview.* This is a twelve-week course and a wonderful, thorough initiation into the arena of worldview thinking. Each of the ten academic areas I mentioned before is covered: theology, philosophy, biology, psychology, ethics, sociology, law, politics, economics, and history. This book also has an accompanying video that explains the concepts that will be presented in the course.

For parents who have never had worldview training, I strongly encourage you to work your way through this material. You need to be able to discuss these ideas with your children, both formally and informally. If your children are young, it helps to have a worldview orientation that serves as a framework for your conversations and your parenting. You will better understand the worldview orientation of movies, television programs, and children's books. Our children desperately need for us to be able to interpret the pop culture that surrounds them. When your children complain about learning the multiplication tables, you will be able to explain that even math is a reflection of God, who has ordered the universe in a careful, calculating manner. As you study the chapter on sociology, you will have a better understanding of the way God designed the institutions of the family, the church, and the state. This chapter will also help you teach each child that he is "not a cog in a machine, he is not a piece of theater; he really can influence history."[26] This course is brimming with rich, powerful information.

If you have teenagers, teach them this material in *Thinking Like a Christian.* If you have never been exposed to the material, you can learn right alongside them. This material is designed to use one on one, in a homeschool co-op, in a youth group, or for an adult Bible study. The accompanying CD in the teacher's textbook will help you customize the material for your particular use. (I have taught this material for high school credit in a homeschool co-op.) You can also purchase a student journal that gives your teens a chance to interact with the material on a daily basis. My daughter benefited significantly from her daily journaling.

You must be able to discuss the world with your teens from a biblical perspective. This material will enable you to do that. After you finish the material in the first course, you can move on to *Countering Culture: Arming Yourself to Confront Non-Biblical Worldviews.*

There are a number of worldview training programs that have been designed for teens. Dr. Noebel, author of the worldview curriculum, is the president and cofounder of Summit Ministries in Colorado Springs. Summit Ministries offers intensive two-week educational conferences (for high school students) that analyze the major humanistic worldviews of our day, contrasting them with the Christian Worldview. Seventy-plus hours of lectures are offered by college professors, authors, and other experts. This training is an excellent way to enable your student to think like a Christian and analyze the culture around him. Additionally, Summit Ministries now offers a program at Bryan College in Tennessee under the leadership of Dr. Jeff Myers.[27]

Patrick Henry College offers summer camps on a wide variety of worldview-related topics.[28] Worldview Academy (WVA) has been providing worldview training for students and their parents since 1996. WVA offers five-day leadership camps for students, as well as Christianity and Culture (weekend) Conferences for parents and students.[29]

When Worldview Training Bears Fruit

You will begin to see the careful cultivation of your child's worldview bear fruit in a number of delightful and sometimes surprising ways. You will see it in their behavior and their spiritual growth. As they get older, you will also notice the fruit in their academic lives and leadership/communication skills. We will discuss this visible fruit in much more detail in chapters 6 through 8.

As my sons moved from a Christian college to a secular campus to finish their undergraduate careers, I was continually amazed at how they could successfully engage their professors in conversations that centered on Christianity. They each had many opportunities to share the gospel in meaningful and creative ways because they could analyze the academic content from a biblical perspective. During one philosophy class, Ty received permission from the professor to debate the existence of God with an agnostic classmate for the entire class period. Ty presented verse after verse, and was able to witness effectively to the entire class. John was concerned in an upper-level literature class about the negative treatment that one author gave Reformation theology. John gained permission from the professor to give the history and meaning of the Reformation from another perspective—and proceeded to give a presentation on the Reformation from a powerful, biblical perspective. At the end of his "lecture," one of the other students asked the professor if the material from John's lecture would be included on the test!

One of the side benefits of working with your children to develop a biblical worldview is the creation of critical thinking skills. These skills will aid your children in a host of academic pursuits, not the least of which is taking the SAT (college boards), which is considered a reasoning test. Remember how important conversation is in the child's developing brain? As you talk constantly with your children about the important issues of life, you are not only strengthening their souls, but building their brain power.

Conclusion

George Barna, while conducting research on the characteristics of young people today, reported that the "alarmingly fast decline of moral foundations among our young people has culminated in a one-word worldview: 'whatever.'"[30] What a passive, disheartening response to life. Our goal for our children as Christian parents stands in complete opposition to this. We want our children to engage and impact the culture, not retreat from it. We want them to use their gifts to glorify God and help others, like Joseph—who saved the land of Egypt from famine while refusing to compromise his religious beliefs. Or Daniel, who read the handwriting on the wall for King Belshazzar (when no one else could), governed wisely, and refused to compromise his religious beliefs even when his life was threatened.

While their "whatever" peers are apathetic and withdrawing from culture, we want our children to enthusiastically and energetically use their God-given gifts and potential to redemptively serve the culture. While others whimper "whatever," we wait expectantly to hear our children reverently—but confidently—yell, "Charge!"

chapter six

TOOL NUMBER 5

building character
through discipleship

a s homeschooling grew in South Carolina, I was asked to represent the homeschooling viewpoint in a number of different
and rather unique forums. On one occasion, I participated in a "blue-
ribbon" panel on education, held at one of our colleges. This consor-
tium included a number of community leaders addressing different
aspects of public education: we were all asked to address problems
with public education, and were each given three minutes to do it.

Speaking on homeschooling is one of my passions in life—it is a privilege and pleasure that I cherish. For some reason, however, I was unusually apprehensive about this particular speaking engagement, sensing that this group could be particularly hostile. I called my dad and asked him if he would go with me. I knew that he would know many of the people in attendance, and it made me feel better just knowing that he would be there.

When we arrived at the meeting, Dad started making the rounds, shaking hands with everyone he knew—attorneys, civic leaders, and others. I made my way to the front, where the tables were set up for the presenters. I sat down, feeling a little anxious as I surveyed the crowd, trying to identify which groups were represented, and looking for a single friendly face.

As the meeting was getting ready to start, Dad walked to the speakers' table, leaned over it, gave me a quick hug, and then helped me get my papers and materials in order. In effect, he was saying to that roomful of people, "This is my daughter; treat her with respect or you'll answer to me."

As he walked away, the words from Psalm 23 encompassed me, resonating deep within: "You prepare a table before me in the presence of my enemies" (v. 5). All of a sudden it didn't matter to me what anyone else in that room thought of me, homeschooling, or what I had to say that day. I only cared about my dad. I wanted him to be proud of me. His presence filled me with confidence and strength as I stood up to speak.

The Heart of Discipleship

This is the heart of discipleship—helping our children reach the point in their lives where they are concerned first and foremost with what the Father thinks and are trying to please Him in all that they are and do. Helping our children develop their own relationship with their Heavenly Father is the goal of discipleship in our homes as we teach them daily what it means to be sons and daughters of the King. Our goal is to take their hands and place them in the Father's hand. Of course, we also teach them that it is only because of the death and resurrection of Christ that they have access to the Father.

The Role of Parents in Discipleship

In the Great Commission Jesus tells us: "All authority has been given to Me in heaven and on earth. Go, therefore, and make disciples of all nations, baptizing them in the name of the Father and of the Son and of the Holy Spirit, teaching them to observe everything I have commanded you. And remember, I am with you always, to the end of the age." Surely this command applies to parents and their children. Our children should be number one on our priority list of making disciples. To make disciples we must first make sure we understand what a disciple is. The Greek word for disciple is *matheteuo*. One of the definitions for this word is, "One who engages in learning through instruction from another."[1]

This definition demystifies the process of discipleship. Discipling is simply instructing another person. In this case, we as parents are teaching our children. The Greek definition encourages us to make our instruction interesting, inviting, discernible, and applicable, so that the students (our children) become actively and eagerly engaged in what we are trying to teach. Our discipleship has two goals: we want our children to love God the Father and to be conformed to the image of Jesus Christ (to have Christ-like character). Additionally, as we discussed in chapter 5, true discipleship will encourage our children as they grow older and mature spiritually and emotionally, to engage and impact the culture for Christ rather than withdraw from the world around them.

When we take the time to establish identity, cultivate intimacy, discover individual purpose, and develop a biblical worldview in our children's lives, we are discipling them. Chapters 7 and 8 deal with providing stimulating academics for our children and fostering leadership and communication skills in our children. These activities are also part of the discipleship process.

In this chapter we will look at several other aspects of discipleship:

- Connecting our children to their Heavenly Father
- Recognizing God's role in the discipleship of our children
- Teaching our children to remember God in their daily lives
- Analyzing why Americans have forgotten how to raise healthy children—spiritually, emotionally, and morally

- Teaching our children the principles and priorities that are important to God, which include Loving God and Loving our neighbors through service, good manners, and good behavior

As parents we bear great responsibility in teaching (discipling) our children. Luke 6:40 reminds us, "A disciple is not above his teacher, but everyone who is fully trained will be like his teacher." This verse grips me. If I fully train my children, they will be like me. Therefore, if I want them to love God and have Christ-like character, I had better make my personal goals loving God and having Christ-like character.

This verse from Luke drives me to prayer and throws me on the mercy of God. It also reminds me of my favorite verse in Scripture about parenting. "Furthermore, we had natural fathers discipline us, and we respected them. Shouldn't we submit even more to the Father of spirits and live? For they disciplined us for a short time based on what seemed good to them, but He does it for our benefit, so that we can share His holiness" (Heb. 12:9–10).

God knows us and understands that we are but dust. He knows we do the best we can as parents, but only He is a perfect parent. He undertakes for us and helps us as parents, and He is active in the lives of our children, training and disciplining them perfectly when they need it.

The Role of the Heavenly Father in Discipleship

When our children believe in Christ, they become sons and daughters of God. "But when the completion of the time came, God sent His Son, born of a woman, born under the law, to redeem those under the law, so that we might receive adoption as sons. And because you are sons, God has sent the Spirit of His Son into our hearts, crying, 'Abba, Father!' So you are no longer a slave, but a son; and if a son, then an heir through God" (Gal. 4:4–7). That term *Abba* in this verse means "daddy." It is a very intimate term.

The privileges of sonship are accompanied by great responsibilities. I have always known, without a doubt, how much my father loves me. Growing up, I also had a very healthy respect for his authority, knowing his very high standards for and expectations of his children. The same responsibilities of sonship also accompany God's unconditional love for us. We can count on the fact that God will exhort us and discipline us as we need it. He wants us to act like His children. As our children come to a saving faith in Christ, God will also treat them like sons. He will love them, affirm them, help them, and discipline them. "My son, do not take the Lord's discipline lightly, or faint when you are reproved by Him; for the Lord disciplines the one He loves, and punishes every son whom He receives. Endure it as discipline: God is dealing with you as sons. For what son is there whom a father does not discipline? . . . No discipline seems enjoyable at the time, but painful. Later on, however, it yields the fruit of peace and righteousness to those who have been trained by it" (Heb. 12:5–7, 11).

God's discipline of us and our children results in righteousness, which is manifested in growing character. God wants us to act like children of the King. He wants our motivations and behavior to be noble. He does not shield us from difficult tasks; as a matter of fact, according to Oswald Chambers, God often gives us difficult tasks to conform us more and more into the image of His Son Jesus. God's discipline, along with the assignments He brings into each child's life, will develop character.

If we are going to live as disciples of Jesus, we have to remember that all noble things are difficult. The Christian life is gloriously difficult, but the difficulty of it does not make us faint and cave in, it rouses us up to overcome. Do we so appreciate the marvelous salvation of Jesus Christ that we are our utmost for His highest?

Thank God He does give us difficult things to do! His salvation is a glad thing, but it is also a heroic, holy thing. It tests us for all we are worth. Jesus is bringing many "sons" unto glory, and God will not shield us from the requirements of a son. God's grace turns out men and women with a strong family likeness to Jesus Christ, not milksops. It takes a tremendous amount of discipline to live the noble life of a disciple of Jesus in actual things. It is always necessary to make an effort to be noble.[2]

Remembering God

As members of the South Carolina Association of Independent Home Schools (SCAIHS), all parents are asked to name their homeschool. Dr. Steve Suits, who served as board chairman while I was president, named his school *Coram Deo,* which means "in the face of God." The name of our school, on the other hand, was the quite plain Tyler School for Boys. What made this name even worse is that we kept it even after Lizzy became school age. As I searched for a new name that had some deeper meaning, I asked Steve how he came up with such a powerful name. All he said was, "You'll know it when the right name comes along."

Lizzy and I were up late one Monday night working on a project she had due for Excelsior! Academy the next day. (One of the benefits of homeschooling co-ops, tutorials, and classes is the presence of unyielding deadlines.) Part of the assignment included researching our family coats of arms. I had a coat of arms for both the Tyler and the Peters (my family) sides of the family. Lizzy and I read together the explanations on the back of each of the coats of arms: the colors used, the meaning of the various symbols, some family history, and the family mottoes. The motto on the Peters's coat of arms jumped out at us: "Rien sans Dieu." It means "Nothing without God." As Lizzy and I discussed the significance of the motto, I immediately knew it should become the name of our school.

God wants us to remember Him. Part of remembering Him is realizing where we would be and what we would have without Him—

remembering that we are nothing without God. In chapter 2, we talked about what happens to societies that forget God—they become random and purposeless. We have also discussed Deuteronomy 6:6–7 on a couple of occasions: "Repeat them [these words] to your children. Talk about them when you sit in your house and when you walk along the road, when you lie down and when you get up." God commands us to talk about Him constantly with our children so that they will remember Him as they move through the normal routines of daily life.

The Scriptures are full of admonitions about remembering God. Read the following verses to your children and discuss what it means to remember God as we live our daily lives. Note that sometimes God exhorts us to remember who He is; other times He tells us to remember what He has done. (In the following verses, the emphases are mine).

- "You shall well *remember what the* LORD *your God did* to Pharaoh and to all Egypt" (Deut. 7:18 NASB).

- "But you shall *remember the* LORD *your God,* for it is He who is giving you power to make wealth, that He may confirm His covenant which He swore to your fathers, as it is this day" (Deut. 8:18 NASB).

- "*Remember His wonderful deeds* which He has done, His marvels and the judgments from His mouth" (1 Chron. 16:12 NASB).

- "When I saw their fear, I rose and spoke to the nobles, the officials and the rest of the people: 'Do not be afraid of them; *remember the Lord who is great and awesome'*" (Neh. 4:14 NASB).

- *"Remember also your Creator in the days of your youth,* before the evil days come and the years draw near when you will say, 'I have no delight in them'" (Eccles. 12:1 NASB).
- *"Remember Jesus Christ,* risen from the dead, descendant of David, according to my gospel" (2 Tim. 2:8 NASB).
- "And when He had given thanks, He broke it and said, 'This is My body, which is for you; *do this in remembrance of Me.'* In the same way He took the cup also after supper, saying, 'This cup is the new covenant in My blood; do this, as often as you drink it, *in remembrance of Me'"* (1 Cor. 11:24–25 NASB).

"America has forgotten how to raise healthy kids."[3]

This pronouncement made by Peter L. Benson, president of the Search Institute, stemmed from research by that organization that culminated in *The Troubled Journey.* This report studied fifty thousand sixth-through-twelfth graders from small, Midwestern communities. More than 80 percent of the youths came from intact families. These are children who should be healthy emotionally, yet of those studied, "only one in ten met a set of criteria for 'optimal healthy development.'"[4]

The news gets worse. In 1998, Patricia Hersch wrote her seminal work *A Tribe Apart: A Journey into the Heart of American Adolescence.* She spent several years with eight adolescents in middle school through high school, staying immersed in their lives, in order to more fully understand the adolescent culture and its pressures. Her insights are revealing. The following two are just a sampling:

1. "Adults, burned out by the years of day care arrangements, are happy the kids are old enough to be on their own. Besides, most believe adolescents prefer being left alone. . . . Aloneness makes adolescents a tribe apart."[5]

2. In an "Ethical Decision Making in the Workplace and Society" seminar, Hersch says this about the roomful of high school seniors, "The room is frighteningly devoid of conscience."[6]

Could it possibly be that our collective societal amnesia on how to raise healthy kids stems from collectively forgetting God? Parents who forget God often forget their children as well in the midst of other pursuits. When we forget to talk about God and His Word to our children, as Deuteronomy 6:6–7 commands, we develop no spiritual identity or intimacy with our children. When we forget to tell them, "Do not murder, do not commit adultery, do not steal, do not covet," we shouldn't be surprised when they do these things. Forgotten children often exhibit behavior (a lack of character) that is costly to society.

Consider the following dismal statistics, and remember that this was fifteen years ago. Our youth culture has certainly not improved since then.

As early as 1989, *Turning Points: Preparing American Youth for the Twenty-first Century* warned that by age 15, substantial numbers of American youth are at risk of reaching adulthood unable to meet adequately the requirements of the workplace, the commitments of relationships in families and with friends, and the responsibilities of participation in a democratic society. These youths are among the estimated 7 million young people—one in four adolescents—who are extremely vulnerable to multiple high-risk behaviors and school failure. Another 7 million may be at moderate risk. . . .[7]

In other words, *half* of all America's adolescents are at some risk for serious problems like substance abuse; early, unprotected sexual intercourse; dangerous, accident-prone behavior; and dropping out of school. The report concluded that today's children are susceptible to a "vortex of new risks . . . almost unknown to their parents or grandparents."[8]

If we want our children to bear fruit upward, we must continue to carefully cultivate our children's potential, even—especially—when they are adolescents. These comments from *A Tribe Apart* corroborate the scriptural principles we have been studying. Our children need us to actively participate in their lives. They need the identity our families give them; they need intimate relationships—so they know they are not alone. They need to understand who they are and how God bent them, and they need the focus and bearings that only a biblical worldview can provide. We must mentor and disciple our children—day by day, precept by precept. As we teach them to remember God—as we teach them what is important to

God—they will be developing the basis for strong character that will follow them throughout their lives.

What Is Important to God?

If we are serious about discipling our children in a way that pleases God, we must focus on those principles and actions that are most significant to Him. Jesus gave us keen insight into His priorities when a Pharisee asked Him which commandment is the greatest. Jesus gave him a two-part answer in Matthew 22:37–40:

- First "Love the Lord your God with all your heart, with all your soul, and with all your mind. This is the greatest and most important commandment" (vv. 37–38).
- "The second is like it: Love your neighbor as yourself. All the Law and the Prophets depend on these two commandments" (vv. 39–40).

LOVE GOD

When Moses went to see Pharaoh about the deliverance of the Israelites from the bondage of slavery, the Lord gave him specific instructions about what to say. Exodus 8:20 tells us this: "The LORD said to Moses, 'Get up early in the morning and present yourself to Pharaoh when you see him going out to the water. Tell him: This is what the LORD says: Let my people go, so that they may worship Me.'"

145

The Lord had a specific reason for delivering the Israelites from slavery: He wanted them to be free to worship Him. Our worship is important to God. He wants our undivided love and worship, and He will go to great lengths to secure both. Look at the strategy of plagues He engineered to finally convince Pharaoh to let His people go. Then, after Pharaoh changed his mind about letting the Israelites go, God remarkably parted the Red Sea to ensure the freedom of His people to worship and serve Him.

We must raise our children to have a knowledge of the importance of worship, as well as teach them how to live in an attitude of worship. The Hebrew word for worship means "bow down."[9] As we contemplate God's love and sacrifice for us through Christ, our automatic response should be to bow before Him—to love and adore Him. We talked about our work being a sacred activity or calling when we offer it to God and do it for His glory. That is worship. When children obey their parents, as unto the Lord, that is worship. When we pray throughout the day, that is worship. Then there are formal times of individual worship, family devotions, and corporate (church) worship. Commitment to a local church is an essential part of discipleship training for our children. The church is referred to as the bride of Christ, signifying its importance to Him. Additionally, Hebrews 10:24–25 admonishes us: "And let us be concerned about one another in order to promote love and good works, not staying away from our meetings, as some habitually do, but encouraging each other, and all the more as you see the day drawing near." Many of the ideas we discuss for service in this chapter and leadership in chapter 8 can occur naturally within the church community.

When we teach our children the importance of living in an attitude of worship, we are teaching them to love God with all their heart, soul, and mind. Sometimes it is good in our society to emphasize to our children that worship involves our minds as well as our emotions. In the chapter on worldview development, we discussed the reasons for this at great length. As our children study and work, the idea of the unity of the sacred and the secular should be ever present, so whatever they do, whether they eat or drink, they do it all to the glory of God.

At one point, one of Lizzy's friends was chastising her for not being involved in more Bible studies outside of her normal church involvement, which is significant. Lizzy finally looked at her friend and said, "Karen, my entire school day is a Bible study." Lizzy meant that whether she is studying a theological tome or a secular piece of literature, she is seeking to integrate her Christianity into every aspect of her studies. That is loving God with "all your mind."

LOVE YOUR NEIGHBOR

In the following section, we will discuss three specific ways that our children can show love to their neighbors: service, good manners, and respectful behavior.

Service

According to Jesus, serving our neighbor is not optional. As we teach our children to put the needs of others before their own, we are teaching them the truth of 1 Peter 3:8–9—that we are here to be a blessing to others, regardless of how they treat us. George Washington Carver's life epitomized this truth. Carver, one of the world's greatest agricultural chemists, is best known for discovering a multitude of uses for peanuts, sweet potatoes, soybeans, and pecans. His work helped revitalize the ailing economy of the South. Continual cotton growth had depleted the southern soil; all of the crops Carver promoted helped to replenish it.[10] Carver was also a committed Christian who made it his goal in life to serve others:

> My purpose alone must be God's purpose—to increase the welfare and happiness of His people. Nature will not permit a vacuum. It will be filled with something. Human need is really a great vacuum which God seeks to fill. . . . With one hand in the hand of a fellow man in need and the other in the hand of Christ, He could get across the vacuum and I became an agent. Then the passage, "I can do all things through Christ which strengtheneth me," came to have new meaning. As I worked on projects which fulfilled a real human need, forces were working through me which amazed me. I would often go to sleep with an apparently insoluble problem. When I woke, the answer was there.[11]

As Carver's fame grew, he was offered lucrative positions by Henry Ford and Thomas Edison, both of which he turned down to continue his research. This man truly employed a thoroughly biblical worldview in his service—he used the gifts God had given him to serve humanity, and he also constantly recognized God as the giver of the gifts. I cannot leave this humble man's life without recounting for you his 1921 testimony before the United States Senate Ways and Means Committee concerning the use of his agricultural discoveries to improve the economy of the South and the lives of her people. The chairman of the committee, enthralled with Carver, extended his time from ten minutes to an hour and forty-five minutes. Here is the exchange that occurred between Carver and the chairman at the end of his address:

> "Dr. Carver, how did you learn all of these things?"
>
> Carver answered: "From an old book."
>
> "What book?" asked the Senator.
>
> Carver replied, "The Bible."
>
> The Senator inquired, "Does the Bible tell about peanuts?"
>
> "No, Sir," Dr. Carver replied, "but it tells about the God who made the peanut. I asked Him to show me what to do with the peanut and He did."[12]

Carver's life bore the hallmarks of biblical service: he humbly put the needs of others before his own; he used his God-given gifts to increase the welfare of others; he used his biblical knowledge and wisdom to help solve significant problems for individuals and society; and in his work and his service, he always acknowledged God. Carver once said, "The secret of my success: It is simple. It is found in the Bible, 'In all thy ways acknowledge Him and He shall direct thy paths.'"[13]

We need to help our children focus on this type of service from the time they are very young. It will help them to grow up creatively seeking to serve God through helping others. To me, this freedom to focus on service as opposed to popularity is one of the great benefits of homeschooling. In a typical school environment, surrounded by peers, a child's tendency is to fit in—to be popular. This escalates to new dimensions during adolescence. At home, we can continually remind our children of Jesus' command to love our neighbors as we love ourselves. If we truly desire to build character into our children's lives, we must be diligent in teaching and training them to serve others. Jesus Himself came to serve, not to be served.

Ideas for service

The flexibility of homeschooling enables you to build service projects and community service into your school day. Most children do not intuitively know how to serve others; we must model service for them and teach them how to serve. We must make service to others a priority in our homes, or more than likely, it will never be a priority for our children.

Some opportunities occur naturally; some take work. When the boys were very young, we had to be creative in finding ways they could serve others without being in the way. Many volunteer organizations do not want younger children around. As I prayed and searched for ways the boys could be meaningfully involved in the lives of others, I kept returning to this verse in the first chapter in James: "Pure and undefiled religion before our God and Father is this: to look after orphans and widows in their distress and to keep oneself unstained by the world" (v. 27). We had many widows in our church, and this seemed like a good place to start. We chose ten to twelve widows to try to serve in a small but meaningful way during the Christmas season.

We actually began working on these Christmas projects, which lovingly became known as "widow baskets," during September of each year. (By starting early, we could complete our projects in time for the Christmas holidays with a minimum of stress and a small time commitment each week.) The boys would memorize a long Scripture passage—twenty or so verses from the Christmas story, for instance—and learn all four verses to a couple of Christmas hymns. We would work on a special art project to include in the baskets; and a month or so before Christmas, we would begin a special cooking project, like making jelly or hot fudge sauce or pies—things that could be stored or frozen and included in the baskets at Christmas. The last Christmas that we made and delivered our baskets, we took them to more than twenty widows, church staff, and neighbors. This turned into a time-consuming project as the boys would recite their verses, sing their songs, and usually give a detailed explanation of every item in the basket. Because these deliveries often turned into extended visits, we could only make one or two deliveries each evening.

In retrospect, the value of these baskets was multifaceted. First, as we added a few more names each year to our list, delivering these baskets became an important focus for our family in December. The boys still had plenty of time to ponder on the things they wanted for Christmas, but this project gave them the opportunity to focus on others instead of focusing exclusively on themselves. Secondly, we talked about Scripture passages that spoke specifically of widows. As we thought of the widowed men and women in our congregation, we prayed for them more; and as we visited them, we developed hearts that were more loving and compassionate. Thirdly, the boys developed strong bonds with many of the older people we visited. As the boys grew up and left home to attend college, these older people in our congregation contributed greatly to their overall prayer support. Twenty years later, many of these relationships are still precious to both Ty and John.

Another Christmas ministry we participated in for many years was Project Angel Tree, a ministry to prison inmates and their children sponsored by Prison Fellowship. In the early years, we were stationed at an island in a mall for hours at a time. I still have visions of the boys handing out fliers to the passersby, explaining why these little children needed Christmas presents.

Joe's parents and my parents have provided important examples of service to the children over the years—through their volunteer work, through their contributions to the community through

various boards and organizations, and through their active involvement in their churches. They have provided the opportunities for Ty,
John, and Lizzy to be involved in many projects that I would not
have had the time for or access to. On many occasions my mother
took us to Charlotte to visit her mother in a nursing home. During
the course of our visits, the children often spent meaningful time
with other people in the home as well. The boys delivered
Thanksgiving meals to needy families with my dad for many, many
years. Through Joe's parents, they have had the opportunity to help
with their church's very large day camp and to serve as counselors at
a camp for the underprivileged. Lizzy has worked with them for the
past several years on Operation Christmas Child—this project, sponsored by Samaritan's Purse, focuses on helping children in war-torn
or impoverished countries during the holidays.

For six years we were involved in tutoring in an inner-city outreach program sponsored by my in-laws' church. My father-in-law,
Ty, John, Lizzy, and I were involved at various levels and in various
capacities. Probably the greatest blessing was developing a relationship with the precious student we tutored and her mother. This
involved about two hours once a week. Tutoring is a great avenue for
service because it is so desperately needed in today's world with our
rising number of functionally illiterate adults and children. As
homeschooling parents, we already know how to tutor. We don't
have to learn any new skills—just employ the ones we already have.
We can also model for the families we're involved with the necessity
of parental involvement in the lives and education of their children.

As Lizzy grew older and her fine arts involvement demanded greater chunks of her time, I thought we would have a more difficult time fitting service into our schedule. It is easy for the tyranny of the urgent to crowd out the really important things. Again the Lord was faithful as we prayed about how to handle this situation. Several of the groups she sang and performed with actually benefited the community. One organization donated a significant portion of the proceeds from its annual performances to Camp Kemo, a program designed to help children with cancer. The Greater Columbia Children's Choir and High School Chamber Choir often sing for hospitals, nursing homes, and churches.

The opportunities to serve others are endless; we just need to begin creatively looking for them. Teens have a variety of options open to them, based on their interests and gifts. Once they are old enough to drive, this frees them to become involved in ministries and organizations without your having to get them there or be there all the time. You still need to thoroughly check out the organizations your teens are involved in, to make sure they are reputable and your teens are safe. I have always known the people my children have worked for in various service and community projects. I want to make sure our goals line up and that they are not going to be mentored by someone whose values compete with ours. I know teens who have been involved in the Special Olympics, Joni and Friends, and Meals-on-Wheels. Many churches and homeschool support groups also have formalized service programs in which your children and teens can participate.

Sometimes our children will creatively employ their talents to serve others in ways we parents would never think of. When Ty and John were in their early teens, they developed a physical education program to benefit the homeschooling mothers in our local support group. For two hours on Friday, they reserved a county recreational facility and planned PE activities for children in kindergarten through sixth grade. During the last half hour, the boys made use of the training they had received in Child Evangelism Fellowship and offered a devotional and Bible study for the children. Since they charged a very nominal fee each week (two or three dollars per child), they provided a real service for these mothers. Last year, Lizzy was approached by several mothers who asked her to teach a classical ballet class to their daughters. In this instance, a mother took the responsibility for coordinating all of the logistics, including finding a place to meet and staying in contact with the parents. Lizzy is providing a valuable service for these mothers by charging less than half the price that they would pay at a dance studio for the same class. Most important, Lizzy strives to be a positive role model for the girls, begins each class with a devotional, and carefully chooses the music they use.

Think about your children's giftings and interests. How would they most enjoy serving others? What talents could they use to benefit others? What are your giftings and talents? Do you love to cook or to sew or to organize? Are you a nurse, doctor, computer guru, teacher, builder, or all-around hard worker? Use your natural abilities, talents, and training as the basis for your volunteer work. Then you can really enjoy it. Get your children involved as well. It takes longer, and the end result may not be as pretty, but you will be participating in raising a generation of servants whose priorities are God's priorities. Remember that homeschooling is a means to an end, not an end in itself. Use the increased time you have as a family to minister to the needs of others. You will find yourself truly blessed as you remember it really is more blessed to give than to receive.

I should probably include this one word of warning. Some of your attempts to serve others will work out amazingly well. Others will flop. I can think of a couple of times where we got involved in outreaches to the poor that were mildly disastrous from our perspective. In other words, the people we were trying to help through two well-established organizations were rude and unappreciative. These circumstances provide us a chance to teach our children yet another lesson about service—we do it as unto the Lord. We give a cup of cold water in Jesus' name because we are obeying Him. We need to obey whether or not we see results from our actions.

Good Manners

For the past several years I have been asked to participate in the educational forum of Leadership South Carolina, an intensive leadership training program sponsored by the Institute for Economic and Community Development of Clemson University. The panel for this forum usually consists of a local public school district superintendent; Larry Watt, the executive director of the private school organization in South Carolina; and myself, representing the homeschooling viewpoint. We each speak for ten minutes concerning the educational option we represent, and then we take questions.

Larry Watt, who always does an excellent job, surprised me one year when speaking of the main reasons parents choose to enroll their children in private schools: one reason he mentioned is parents' desire that their children be taught good manners.

Mr. Watt raises an excellent point. Historically in this country, we have viewed the development of manners as an important part of the educational system. Consider this definition of *education* in the 1828 edition of Noah Webster's *An American Dictionary of the English Language* (emphases in the following passage are mine):

> **Education,** n. [L. education] The bringing up, as of a child; instruction; *formation of manners.* Education comprehends all that series of instruction and discipline which is intended to enlighten the understanding, *correct the temper,* and *form the manners and habits of youth,* and fit them for usefulness in their future stations.

We should be teaching our children good manners. It is part of a well-rounded education. This task becomes increasingly difficult in the society in which we find ourselves, where good manners are not always valued. Television and pop culture are two of the leading culprits in the disappearance of manners from our society. Television sitcoms and the new reality programs focus on degrading others rather than building them up. Christianity lies at the heart of good manners. In Matthew 7:12, Jesus says, "Therefore, whatever you want others to do for you, do also the same for them—this is the Law and the Prophets."

My parents made manners a high priority and demonstrated good manners to my sisters and myself in a thousand different ways while we were growing up. If you did not grow up learning manners or if you feel you need a good resource on how to teach manners to your children, I highly recommend all of June Hines Moore's books on teaching manners and etiquette: *Manners Made Easy: A Workbook for Student, Parent, and Teacher; You Can Raise a Well-Mannered Child;* and *Social Skills Survival Guide.* These books will provide you with the tools you need to teach manners and appropriate behavior to your children.

In *Manners Made Easy: A Workbook for Student, Parent, and Teacher* June Moore says: "My overall goal in writing this workbook/teacher's guide is to enable parents and teachers to motivate their students to learn, and more importantly to practice good manners, gain self-confidence, and try never to embarrass another person or themselves. They [these lessons] will also encourage students to practice the Golden Rule, which is 'Just as you want others to do for you, do the same for them' (Luke 6:31)."[14]

Good Behavior

In a perfect world, if you are raising your children to love God, to serve others, and to exhibit good manners, you should automatically have children who are always well-behaved. As we discussed in chapter 3 (see page 40), the perfect world ended when Adam and Eve sinned and now the world, and everyone in it, is fallen. We are all sinners—everyone, every parent and every child.

Our goal for our children is the same goal that we should have for ourselves: to love Christ and seek to please Him in everything we do—in both our heart attitudes and our outward behavior. I am wary of formulas that promise to produce perfectly behaved children. Discipline, like everything else, takes constant communication, time, and persistence. Glenn Stanton observes: "One of the biggest obstacles that keeps us from being authentic and effective in most things—including family life—is a feeling that we need to be perfect. Where did we ever get the idea that a good Christian family is a perfect family? Again, we certainly don't find those kinds of families in Scripture. What we do find are graphically human families that are in the process of being slowly pulled into God's redemptive care. Christ's grace and redemption shine in our imperfection."[15]

John Rosemond, child psychologist, author, and syndicated columnist, wrote an article entitled "Living with Children," in which he discusses matters of discipline:

> According to Judeo-Christian scripture, misbehavior
> can be controlled, never completely prevented. So, when
> one of Grandma's kids misbehaved, she didn't feel guilty.
> Quite the contrary, she made the offending child feel
> guilty. The *nouveau psychological view,* on the other hand,
> presumes that the misbehaving child is "acting out" some

stress-producing defect in his family. However unwittingly, his parents have made him insecure, or angry, or
caused his self-esteem to drop. So, when today's child mis-
behaves, today's "secularized" parent (again, usually Mom)
is likely to hear a voice in the back of her head saying, "It
might be you!"

Homeschooling is the fastest-growing educational
movement in the nation. Today, some 1.5 million of
America's kids are beings schooled at home, a five-fold
increase over the last eight years. Invariably, the homeschoolers with whom I speak tell me that not only are
their children doing better academically, but also the
family unit is strengthened and the children are better
behaved.[16]

In the first five chapters of this book, we have devoted much of
our discussion to the parents' responsibilities in the home. This
excerpt from Dr. Rosemond's column brings us to the other side of
the equation. Just as parents are responsible before God for their
actions, so are our children. As parents, we want to give our children
every opportunity to succeed and behave correctly. We want to help
them and encourage them to do what is right. That is what the
seven tools are all about. Yet we must remember that, just like us,
our children will sometimes make poor choices and decisions in
life—they will disobey God and their parents.

Paul sums it up best in Ephesians 6:1–4 with verses that carry
words of admonition for both child and parent: "Children, obey your

parents in the Lord, because this is right. Honor your father and mother—which is the first commandment with a promise—that it may go well with you and that you may have a long life in the land. And fathers, don't stir up anger in your children, but bring them up in the training and instruction of the Lord."

Effective discipline requires that husbands and wives work prayerfully and cooperatively together. Discipline cannot be haphazard. You must have a plan that you implement daily in your home. Books abound on the topic of disciplining children. If, as a couple, you need help in effectively disciplining your children, I would encourage you to ask your pastor, church leaders, or a trusted Christian friend to recommend biblical books and resources.

Extended Family

I can't leave this chapter without discussing the important role that extended family can play in discipling and mentoring our children. We live in a mobile society, and many children are raised geographicly apart from grandparents, aunts, uncles, and cousins. Wherever you live, remember that God created us to live in the context of families. The extended family is an important part of that context. Grandparents provide a sense of stability, security, and accountability that all children need. Joe's parents and my parents have reinforced the things we have tried to teach our children. Ty said it best one day: "Boy, Mom, if I mess up, I'm not just letting you and Dad down, I'm also disappointing Grandmayme and

Granddaddy and Ma[16] and Papa." All four of our parents have added an extra dimension to our children's lives—spiritually, morally, emotionally, and socially. They have been an extra measure of protection—a safety net—as our children have maneuvered the sometimes dangerous high-wire of growing up.

Your extended family situation will be unique. Joe and I are particularly blessed to have wonderful families. I have talked with many people who fear abuse or moral problems from members of their extended family. You will need to pray and use your sanctified common sense to know which relationships to nurture and which to avoid.

Wherever possible, however, I would encourage you to connect with your parents and in-laws and other extended family members for your children's sake. I have one friend whose mother teaches his children weekly piano lessons even though they are thousands of miles apart—the wonders of technology. E-mail, cell phones, and cheap long distance rates make it much easier to keep in contact than it ever has been before. If you have no extended family, I would encourage you to find some "adopted" grandparents for your children in your church. Children benefit from interaction with a wide variety of ages.

chapter seven

tool number 6

providing stimulating academics

I n a frantic attempt to avoid boarding the school bus, Dennis the Menace exclaims to his mother, "Margaret said some moms homeschool their kids!"[1]

In an article written for the *Wall Street Journal,* Marvin Olasky, editor of *World Magazine,* said, "The Bible-based revivals that have transformed American culture have had at least three ingredients: an increased sense of God's holiness; an increased knowledge of man's sin and need for a savior; and radical changes in behavior." Olasky goes on to articulate one example of a radical change in behavior: "Conservative Christians are having more children and teaching them at home."[2]

Dr. Allan Carlson, president of The Howard Center for Family, Religion and Society, credits homeschooling with changing the landscape of American education: "Homeschoolers are reinventing both American teaching and American learning," he says, "and the children excel. By grade eight, these children are, on average, almost four years ahead of their public and private school counterparts."[3]

In a 1998 address to the National Christian Home School Leadership Summit in Washington, D.C., Congressman Bill Goodling, former chairman of the powerful Education and Workforce Committee in the U.S. House of Representatives, said this: "The homeschoolers are the most effective lobbyists. You have heard the saying, 'When E. F. Hutton speaks, people listen.' I have changed that saying around a little bit. I say, 'When the home-schoolers speak, you better listen!'"[4]

Homeschooling is reshaping America—from comic strips to behavior to education to politics. Why? God ordained the family to be a strong, defining tool in the lives of individuals and the histories of nations. Families are to be places of learning and of industry. Places for nurturing and encouraging faith. Places of power and significance.

In his speech "How Homeschooling Strengthens Families," Dr. Carlson explains it this way: "Home education . . . represents the return of a central function to the family. And as I suggested earlier, it also forces a fundamental reorganization of the family: in terms of the behavior of all its members, its relationship to the outside world, and its internal psychology. In short, homeschooling families discover what it feels like to be 'reinstitutionalized,' to become strong again, all by bringing a central family function home again."[5] In other words, homeschooling strengthens families by providing a renewed sense of purpose and mission.

Help in a Hurting World

The following e-mail graced my in-box just a few days ago:

> I will be traveling this weekend to Leon, QTO, Mexico, to speak at a church of 300. The pastor called me and said, "We are losing our children. Will you come and teach us how to home school?" Please pray that God will use the three days of teaching to help and encourage the believers at this church.
> Mike Richardson

Mike Richardson was a successful CPA and chief financial officer for a large boat anchor and boat trailer manufacturer until 1993, when he and his wife heard the call to sell everything they had and serve the Lord as full-time missionaries in Mexico. In addition to planting and pastoring a church, Mike has begun a homeschool ministry that reaches families in twenty-nine countries, including Mexico. (Mike's e-mail address is vnm@direcway.com.) Mike publishes *El Hogar*

Educador, a bi-monthly homeschooling magazine with a circulation of almost four thousand. The Richardsons are uniquely qualified to do this—Mike and his wife, Pam, have nine children that they home-school or have homeschooled (three are now grown).

Like this pastor in Mexico, more and more people are realizing homeschooling is powerful and effective, not only in its academic outcomes, but also as a prescription for what ails the family.

The *Home* in Homeschooling

I have deliberately devoted the great majority of this book to the important work that takes place in our homes. The *home* in home-schooling is an essential part of the overall equation. When the home is functioning optimally, the "schooling" occurs much more natu-rally. If you have worked on tools one through five, you have already done the foundational work for tool number six, which is "providing stimulating academics." (For those of you who are considering or have just begun homeschooling, I ask that for a few minutes you set your reservations or fears aside and ponder with me the "schooling" part of the homeschooling equation.)

The Main Ingredients of Stimulating Academics

When children are loved and nurtured, when their potential is cultivated, education becomes infinitely simpler, more efficient, more compelling, and more stimulating. For our purposes, we will discuss five major ingredients in the educational equation: the teacher, time, the classroom or the learning environment, curriculum, and the student.

THE TEACHER

The most powerful characteristics the homeschooling mother brings to the task of teaching are her knowledge of her students and her love for her students. Here is just a sampling of the breadth of her knowledge:

- She knows the students in the context of their family background.
- She knows the bent of each child sitting before her.
- She knows the personality type, the spiritual gifts, the learning style, and the passions of each one.
- She has conversed constantly with these children and invested herself heavily in their health, mental development, and overall well-being.
- She has labored in prayer over each child and asked God to bless each one.
- She has taught these children to love God and to care about one another.
- She has sought specific ways to affirm each child.
- She is intimately acquainted with the problems each child faces—the sin and encumbrances that cling to and entangle

him, threatening his ability to "run with patient endurance and steady and active persistence the appointed course of the race that is set before" him.

Love for the Students

The homeschooling mother is not hired; what she does is a labor of love. Consider John 10:11–12: "I am the good shepherd. The good shepherd lays down his life for the sheep. The hired man, since he is not the shepherd and doesn't own the sheep, leaves them and runs away when he sees a wolf coming." Mothers make great teachers. They are totally committed to stimulating their children academically, regardless of what it requires of them personally. No one rivals the tenacity of a mother when it comes to caring for and educating her children. As my mother always told me, "There is no magic to teaching; it is just hard work."

Sam B. Peavey, Ed.D., corroborates the effectiveness of parents as teachers: "It has been most interesting to me to see homeschool parents with high school diplomas doing as well or better than my certified teachers as measured by their students' standardized test results. Those parents revealed some things to me about living, loving, and learning that I was never taught by my distinguished professors at Harvard and Columbia."[6]

The Power of Companionship and One-on-One Instruction

Homeschooling is efficient and effective because it employs the tutorial method of teaching. The intimate knowledge the homeschooling mother possesses of each student makes this one-on-one instruction even more powerful and compelling. In chapter 3, we discussed the use of personal presence in developing intimacy. Personal presence is also a powerful teaching tool. Robert Frost, the poet and recipient of four Pulitzer Prizes, was a homeschooling parent.[7] He believed in "education by presence": "By 'education by presence,' Frost clearly meant education by example, not education by exhortation. He meant doing, not merely verbalizing. He meant showing, not just telling."[8]

Two verses give insight into how the Lord teaches us. These verses indicate that the Lord's instruction for us is personal and individualized.

1. "I will instruct you and show you the way to go; with My eye on you, I will give counsel" (Ps. 32:8).

2. ". . . but your Teacher will not hide Himself any longer. Your eyes will see your Teacher, and whenever you turn to the right or to the left, your ears will hear this command behind you: 'This is the way. Walk in it'" (Isa. 30:20–21).

Jesus always has His eye on us and gives constant direction. We should make it our goal to emulate Him in the way we teach. This kind of teaching implies constant companionship, which is the heart and soul of homeschooling.

Other Members of the Homeschool Faculty

There have been many times during the course of the past twenty-one years that I have needed help with the teaching load.

I have hired tutors, taken advantage of the classes offered at Excelsior! Academy, or enrolled Ty, John, or Lizzy in a class designed for homeschooled students. Professor Dana Mosely has been our trusted math instructor for upper-level courses for almost ten years through his Chalk Dust video program (www.chalkdust.com). These teachers have become the adjunct faculty for the *Rien sans Dieu* Homeschool Academy.

My husband, Joe, wears many hats. In addition to being the principal and chief financial officer, he serves as the computer teacher, the information technology consultant, and the resident nature specialist. He is also in charge of PE, recreation, attitude adjustment, and comic relief. My parents and Joe's parents have likewise pitched in to help in various capacities throughout the years. Very few people can handle all of the demands of the homeschooling lifestyle without help of some type. Don't be afraid to seek help when you or your child needs it. Commit your need and requests to the Lord. He will do exceeding abundantly beyond all that you can ask or think. "Now without faith it is impossible to please God, for the one who draws near to Him must believe that He exists and rewards those who seek Him" (Heb. 11:6).

TIME

When Joe and I first decided to homeschool Ty in 1984, our plans were to only homeschool him one year. As we finished that first year, I was so pleased and fascinated by what was happening in our home that—in spite of all our legal difficulties—I really wanted to home-school another year. We were growing closer and working together more effectively as a family. This surprised me because I had always been a stay-at-home mom; we had always had plenty of time together, I thought. While the boys had been in preschool and kindergarten, it had only been half days; but half-days notwithstanding, we saw remarkable gains in our family life once we began homeschooling.

In the end, one of the main reasons I resisted putting Ty into a traditional elementary school that second year was the chunk of time school would take him away from the rest of the family. School takes a child's best time. After he stays for extracurricular activities and then does homework, sometimes there is little time left for family life. Teacher John Taylor Gatto concurs: "No effect of compulsory mass-schooling is more resistant to remedy than the damage it has done to the American family by separating parents and kids."[9]

Homeschooling redeems a great deal of time that would be lost in your child's day if he were in school. The efficiency of home-schooling is a great benefit for your children. They can finish their schoolwork more quickly, they are not saddled with hours of home-work, and therefore they have the time to devote to service at church or in the community and to pursue particular interests and passions in life, without disappearing from the landscape of family life.

Dr. David Edgren, former headmaster of Ben Lippen School, wrote this in the school's quarterly newsletter:

> Whatever we think of the homeschooling phenomenon,
> we'd better learn why so many reasonable and intelligent

people are choosing this approach. . . . I'd like to suggest three things we can learn from the success of homeschooling. First, homeschooling engages the learner and focuses on the individual. Consider the diagram below which shows how much serious learning occurs in public and private schools on a typical day.

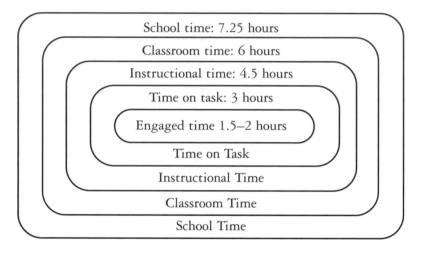

School time: 7.25 hours
Classroom time: 6 hours
Instructional time: 4.5 hours
Time on task: 3 hours
Engaged time 1.5–2 hours
Time on Task
Instructional Time
Classroom Time
School Time

School time: That period of time encompassing the hours that the student is actually in the school building

Classroom time: Time which the student actually spends in the classroom

Instructional time: That portion of the day actually spent on instruction (subtract such things as small talk, housekeeping, attendance, interruptions, assemblies, posturing, discipline, etc.)

Time on task: Time in which the student is apparently listening, reading his text, writing something down, paying attention, playing by the rules, etc.

Engaged time: Time in which the learner is actively engaged in learning: his mind is in gear; he is with the teacher on the task with all of his energy

Why do we say to our children and to our students: "Look at me, give me your eyes?" We want them to be engaged with us. When our family . . . homeschooled . . . we found that we could accomplish in two hours what the school, any school, could do the entire school day. It has a lot to do with engaged time. . . . Homeschooling by no means ensures this kind of engagement, but it is exceedingly more likely in this setting than in traditional schooling.[10]

THE CLASSROOM AND LEARNING ENVIRONMENT

The two most important components of your classroom are dynamics and resources. By dynamics I mean the interactions and energy in your home. We have spent the first six chapters discussing these—the first five tools are your key to providing a positive, stimulating learning environment. Consider especially the discussion we had on *conversation* in chapter 3. Conversation and personal interaction will be a significant builder of academic ability and success in your home.

Remember two points from our previous discussion of "conversation as core curriculum":

- Christian homes should be the protectors and propagators of language in our "linguistically malnourished" society. Our homes should be environments bursting with language.

- Recall these words from the book *Endangered Minds*: "I think it would be very important to tell parents they are participating with the physical development of their youngsters' brain to the exact degree that they interact with them, communicate with them. Language interaction is actually building tissue in their brains—so it's also helping build youngsters' futures."[11]

In the homeschool environment, dialog and constant interactions are the norm. Personal interactions with each child can number in the hundreds daily. In the traditional classroom environment, the child has very limited personal interaction with the teacher, probably averaging about eight to ten times a day.

The emotional environment is also an important part of the dynamics of the learning environment in your home. Henry Ward Beecher, a pastor in the 1800s and brother of Harriet Beecher Stowe, said, "The mother's heart is the child's school-room."[12] What is in your heart will impact your children. If you enjoy homeschooling, your children will more than likely enjoy homeschooling. Robert Frost also weighs in on this topic: "Frost maintained an approach to teaching which favored involvement and enjoyment rather than scholarship and criticism."[13] You will have good days and bad days in your homeschool, and days when your children are more cooperative than others. But if you will make the effort to be optimistic, enthusiastic, and affirming, you will be sowing good things into the soil of your child's heart, and this will bear good fruit in your children's lives—although you might not see that fruit immediately or every day. Remember the verses from Galatians 6:9–10: "So we must not get tired of doing good, for we will reap at the proper time if we don't give up. Therefore, as we have opportunity, we must work for the good of all, especially for those who belong to the household of faith."

As you think of resources in your classroom, learn to think of your home as the hub that provides your students ready access to your *real* classroom—the world. For homeschooling families, the world truly becomes your classroom through field trips, daily outings, the great outdoors, family visits, travel opportunities, missions trips, internships, and lots of reading. Don't forget to equip each child with a public library card—giving him access to some of the best libraries in the world.

CURRICULUM

One of the themes of this book has been that of curriculum; but rather than speaking of textbooks and subjects, we have spoken of curriculum as the unique course that God has developed and appointed for each of our children to run. Right now, however, we need to talk for just a few minutes about curriculum in terms of what books to use in the homeschooling process.

The choice of textbooks and curricular material must be made in the greater contexts of who your child is, how he learns, how you learn, what his post-high-school goals include, how many children you are teaching, what your budget is—this list could go on *ad infinitum*. When I began homeschooling, choosing curriculum was not exciting, but it was not difficult either. My choices were limited by products available to homeschoolers, which was not much; I was further restricted by the homeschooling law in my state; and the final limitation was my failure to understand that textbooks aren't the only important educational resources. Now the process of choosing homeschooling curriculum is complicated because there are so many available resources, homeschooling laws are no longer restrictive, and more information is available on the creative use of resources of all kinds.

So, how does a parent choose what to use? Here are four suggestions.

1. I highly recommend Cathy Duffy's book *100 Top Picks for Homeschool Curriculum.* This book will provide solid guidance and specific direction for you as you endeavor to choose stimulating curriculum for your children. This book has a wealth of invaluable information about how and what to choose, and it considers the most important factors that contribute to curriculum selection, including learning styles.[14]

2. Call your state homeschooling organization[15] or local support group and ask if they provide curriculum counseling. If they don't, they might be able to point you toward someone

who does. Some homeschooling organizations, like the South Carolina Association of Independent Home Schools,[16] are designed to provide individualized curriculum counseling to their members. Because of this service, SCAIHS has members across the country, as well as a host of missionaries living around the world.

3. Identify a veteran homeschooler whose family inspires you. Pick her brain and find out what curriculum she has used and why.

4. Go online. The homeschool area of Lifeway.com at www.lifeway.com/homeschool has an entire section devoted to curriculum.

Whatever you choose to use, remember that you are the teacher and the curriculum is the tool. You are the master and it is the slave—not vice versa. You are free to adjust it according to your goals and schedule and your child's needs. There is nothing sacred about completing each and every assignment. Remember that conversation should always be part of your core curriculum. Plan field trips that correspond with the topics of study in your curriculum. Make sure there is plenty of interaction between you and your children.

Other Curriculum Considerations

1. As you choose curriculum and prepare to teach, review the chapter on developing a biblical worldview. Remember the injunction from Harvard's 1646 "Rules and Precepts," to "lay Christ at

the bottom, as the only foundation of all sound knowledge and learning."

Remember the power of the Word of God to work positively and powerfully in your child's life. Because we have become used to education that cannot consider the Bible, we fail to realize what a powerful tool it is in the education of our children. (This subject on its own could fill many volumes.) In both her colonial days and her early days as a nation, America had extremely high literacy rates. Interestingly enough, the Bible played an important role in education during these time periods. In the children's book *Stories of the Pilgrims,* the author made this comment about Edward Winslow, a pilgrim, teaching Squanto, the Indian who taught the Pilgrims to survive in the New World, how to read: "There were no primers or first readers then, but Winslow took down his Bible. It was the book from which he had learned to read; he would teach Squanto from it."[17]

In a children's biography about George Washington Carver, the author tells the story of Carver hearing this verse read in church, "And if some of the branches be broken off, and thou, being a wild olive tree, wert grafted in among them, and with them partakest of the root and fatness of the olive tree . . ." This verse overwhelmed the young Carver and prompted great thought that eventually led to his amazing agricultural and horticultural discoveries.

To remind yourself of the power of God's Word in the education of your children, post these beautiful and powerful words from the Book of Isaiah on your desk or in your planbook:

"For as heaven is higher than earth, so My ways are higher than your ways, and My thoughts than your thoughts. For just as rain and snow fall from heaven, and do not return there without saturating the earth, and making it germinate and sprout, and providing seed to sow and food to eat, *so My word that comes from My mouth will not return to Me empty, but it will accomplish what I please, and will prosper in what I send it {to do}.*" You will indeed go out with joy and be peacefully guided. (Isa. 55:9–12, author emphasis)

2. Consider teaching the principles of good character and character development as part of your core curriculum. Review the chapter on building character through discipleship for suggestions of activities and materials to build into your school day. Curriculum like KONOS arranges its academic instruction around specific character traits.[18] In the midst of his brilliance, Noah Webster, the author of the first American dictionary,[19] recognized the essential aspect of character development within the context of education: "To exterminate our popular vices is a work of far more importance to the character and happiness of our citizens, than any other improvements in our system of education."[20]

3. One of the greatest and most exciting strengths of home-schooling is the freedom and ability to connect learning to life. All of life becomes part of the learning experience—a trip to the nursing home to visit grandparents, a hike in the woods, political discussions around the dining room table, participation in a soccer league, service to the community and church, working in meaningful

internships, participation in a missions trip, and volunteering in a political campaign. All of life stimulates us to learn when viewed this way. Combining traveling and books on tape/CD is a powerful educational tool. I can remember driving home from a trip when the children were ages five to fourteen, listening to Willa Cather's *O! Pioneers* the entire way. When we arrived home at one o'clock in the morning, all three children begged to stay up and listen to the last tape before we went to bed. What a memory—five exhausted travelers sprawled on the bedroom floor listening to the conclusion of an exciting book.

Just like Christians suffer when we compartmentalize our spiritual lives so that the sacred and secular are divided, children suffer when learning is separated from life and meaningful experiences, and is relegated strictly to a classroom.

Gatto sheds some interesting light on this subject from his many years spent as a teacher:

> In centuries past, children and adolescents would
> spend their time in real work, real charity, real adventures,
> and in the search for mentors who might teach them what
> they really wanted to learn. A great deal of time was spent
> in community pursuits, practicing learning how to make a
> home, and performing dozens of other tasks necessary to
> becoming whole men and women. But the children I teach
> have no time for these pursuits. After television, schooling,
> sleeping, and eating, they have only about nine hours each
> week to spend on growing up. Is it any wonder that the

children I teach are indifferent to the adult world, have almost no curiosity, and have a poor sense of the future, of how tomorrow is inextricably linked to today?[21]

Robert Frost agreed, "We don't want much school even when we are young, that is to say, we want a great deal more of life than of school."[22]

These positions do not stand in opposition to academic achievement. Quite the contrary. The intent is to encourage us to fill our children's lives with a rich combination of relationships, books, and experiences that in turn encourage serious, stimulating scholarship.

4. Consider extracurricular activities, along with internships and meaningful work experiences, as part of your curriculum. As you have become students of your children, learning their bents, learning styles, spiritual gifts, and strengths, you can begin to discern which activities will benefit them and which will be wastes of time and even counterproductive. Athletic involvement provided positive activities and opportunities for both Ty and John. Both boys played baseball, basketball, and soccer, and occasionally swam on swim teams.

Joe and I believed that playing sports was beneficial to the boys on a number of different levels:

- The boys stayed in excellent physical shape, and we counted the time as physical education.

- With energetic little boys (and big boys), this was a positive way to expend energy.

- Many of the leagues we participated in were church leagues, and the atmosphere was positive.

- As the boys got older and played in competitive sports leagues, this provided them an opportunity to interact with a wide variety of people. They played sports with many boys who weren't Christians, and this gave them a forum to live out their Christianity—to provide some moral and spiritual leadership—in a place where Christianity was not the normal topic of discussion.

- We attended virtually all of the boys' games, making their sports endeavors a family affair.

- The boys' expertise opened up job and ministry opportunities as they got older. They served as counselors at a Fellowship of Christian Athlete's weeklong soccer camp. John helped coach the girls' soccer team at a Christian high school. Both boys were offered soccer scholarships at the collegiate level. An area pastor asked John to organize and coach a soccer team to take to England and use as a vital part of the church's outreach ministry. When Ty graduated from college, he posted his resumé online. (The resumé included information on playing collegiate soccer.) A recruiter found Ty through this resumé and recommended him for a job because he believed that the discipline and teamwork that is required to play sports at the collegiate level would make him a valuable asset to the company. Ty got the job, and sports were his initial entree.

Our family has been heavily involved politically. We could trace the benefits for those political involvements as we did the sports.

Music has been an important part of John's and Lizzy's lives. (Ty took piano lessons one year because we thought it contributed to his overall education, although music was not a strength.) I would encourage you to assess your children's interests and strengths and decide which types of activities would strengthen their gifts, allow them to contribute to the needs of others, and open doors for them in the future. This is a fluid process. Sometimes you will find great activities, and other times the opportunity you think will be perfect is disappointing. This is part of life and can be as much of a learning experience for your children as something that turns out well. As you commit these areas and decisions to the Lord, He will lead you and guide you and open doors for your children that will amaze you.

THE STUDENT

Now we come to the main point of the chapter—your children as students. Each student is totally unique, and his curriculum ("the appointed course of the race that is set before him") will be different from that of every other student in the world. There is common knowledge, of course, which must be mastered, but a powerful, stimulating education is one that is specifically designed for the individual, and not one-size-fits-all.

Use the diagnostic questions from chapter 4, on discovering purpose, to help you develop the educational plan that best suits your child.

For instance, as I thought about each of my three children, I knew that I wanted them to take college preparatory classes in high school. Within that context, I knew that the same courses had different meanings for Ty, John, and Lizzy. While John and Ty took the same biology and chemistry courses (taught by a homeschooling grandfather who was a retired science teacher), my goals for them were very different because their goals were very different. John wanted to be a dentist and loves science—he needed rigorous training both in lab settings and in lecture. Mr. Staudenbauer's classes filled this need. Ty needed the classes to graduate from high school and go on to college. They contributed to a well-rounded education for him, but I knew that the sciences were not an academic discipline he would pursue with career goals in mind. John also took physics from Mr. Staudenbauer, which Ty didn't need. Mr. Staudenbauer had the credentials I was looking for in a teacher—expertise and credentials in his field and a strong biblical worldview, especially as it pertains to creation.

Lizzy has a strong interest in broadcast journalism. I have tried very hard to determine the courses and skills she would need to pursue her interests. I considered English courses, composition, and speech and debate courses to be foundational. The stage experience she gained from her fine arts pursuits has contributed to her poise and confidence in speaking before audiences. As we prayed for and sought out other opportunities, the Lord was faithful to bring things to us. We found out about a weeklong journalism camp offered at Patrick Henry College. Then Lizzy was offered the opportunity to serve as an intern at WMHK Christian radio station. We counted all these activities as school time and gave her high school credit for these endeavors. These activities also served the purpose in Lizzy's life of confirming that she does indeed enjoy journalism. They very well could have had the opposite effect. In any event, I felt that everything she was doing had educational value—so that the time was well-spent regardless of her final inclinations.

One ultimate goal we should strive toward in our home-schooling is to so kindle our children's love for learning that they become independent, lifelong learners. "Learning," Robert Frost believed, "must be firsthand, and education should both delight and instruct." He sought innovative ways to motivate his students to become independent learners. He said, "I still say the only education worth anything is self-education."[23] Sir Walter Scott said, "All men who have turned out worth anything have had the chief hand in their own education."[24]

Helpful Resources

Time fails us to discuss all the aspects of home education that are important to us as parents, including homeschooling in high school (in-depth), homeschooling children with special needs, home-schooling boys, understanding pertinent legal and political issues, knowing how to get started—the list could go on and on. Here are some specific resources that can help:

For legal information, contact Home School Legal Defense Association at www.hslda.org or by phone at (540) 338-5600.

7 tools *for* CULTIVATING
your child's potential

For more information on the other issues in the list, I invite you to visit the homeschool area of Lifeway.com's Web network at www.lifeway.com/homeschool. We have developed a site devoted to the issues that concern you most: getting started; choosing curriculum; homeschooling in high school; homeschooling special needs; current events, legal, legislative, and political issues that affect homeschooling; and encouragement in a whole host of areas.

Conclusion

God is faithful to direct and superintend our children's educations when we place them in His hands. He often augments our plans with assignments of His own for our children that can include wonderful opportunities as well as difficulties and adversity. He gives our children strengths that He can use in the world; He also gives them weaknesses to keep them humble and reliant on Him. Whatever He does, we can count on the fact that it is perfect.

Homeschooling is an exciting way to educate children. Homeschooling continues to grow because it works academically and socially, it fosters creativity, and it strengthens families. Homeschooling is an excellent educational choice for Christian parents who desire to infuse their children's academic, vocational, and moral training with a strong biblical worldview that has served Western civilization so well throughout the ages.

chapter eight

TOOL NUMBER 7

fostering leadership and communication skills

When John was fourteen, he traveled to Mier y Noriega, a very small town in an impoverished area of Mexico, to participate in a medical missions trip. Dr. Gregg McKenzie, a periodontist, arranged the trip and took his thirteen-year-old son, David, (John's best friend) as his dental assistant. Dr. Ben Jett took John as his dental assistant. When the foursome arrived in Mier y Noriega, they set up shop in a small dusty building. They had few patients the first day; but when word spread that this was painless dentistry, thanks to their supply of lidocaine, the indigent people lined up around their makeshift office in increasing numbers. Most had never seen a dentist and had multiple problems. One man had been in constant pain for many years. When he sat in the dental chair and received the lidocaine injection that numbed his tooth, he thought he had been healed! He hugged the dentists and left in tears. They could not make him understand the relief was only temporary. He was back in a couple of hours.

With just a few days remaining, Dr. Jett showed John how to give injections, pull teeth, surgically remove teeth decayed below the gum line, and stitch up the affected area when necessary. At the age of fourteen John had the unbelievable experience of "doing" dentistry.

This trip was a beneficial and instructive experience for John on many different levels. John was taking Spanish II at the time and, from a language standpoint, this was an incredible opportunity for him to hone and develop his language skills. Although John had been involved in different inner-city ministries, he had never been exposed to the level of abject poverty he witnessed in Mexico. This trip, the first of many missions trips for John, was instrumental in developing within him a growing heart for missions. But the most unanticipated benefit of this trip came in the form of career direction. John wanted to become a dentist. John was profoundly affected by the leadership Dr. McKenzie and Dr. Jett demonstrated in using their professional knowledge to serve the poor and share the gospel.

Right after John's trip, I participated on an educational panel in a neighboring state with a public school administrator and the executive director of a private school association. Because the audience was comprised mainly of career women, I thought there would be very little interest in homeschooling. I was wrong. A question from the audience prompted me to tell the story of John's multifaceted mission trip. As I was talking, the man on the panel representing private schools jumped up and exclaimed excitedly while pointing at me, "Now that's real education! That is applying knowledge to the world around you!"

Cultivation and Leadership

He's right, but this is not only real education. Applying knowledge to improve the lives of others also epitomizes leadership and is the culmination of the message of this book. We carefully cultivate our children's potential for a reason. When they leave our homes, we want them to be equipped to make a difference in this world. As George Washington Carver said, "My purpose alone must be God's purpose—to increase the welfare and happiness of His people."

At the end of this book, we realize we have come full circle. In chapter 1 we discussed the importance of educating our children—of "drawing out the gifts God has given." The concepts of educating our children and cultivating their potential are inextricably linked. As they grow up and leave home, our children will be given the similar task of educating and cultivating the people and the world around them. Remember Colson's words in chapter 5?: "In the opening chapters of Genesis, we learn that human beings were made in the image of God, to reflect his character; therefore, we are called to reflect his creative activity through our own creativity—by cultivating the world, drawing out its potential, and giving it shape and form. All work has dignity as an expression of the divine image."

Because you have focused on cultivating your children's potential and because they have lived in a home that has practiced and modeled this, they should be uniquely equipped in this task of using their creativity and gifts to "cultivate the world and draw out its potential." This is leadership—taking the initiative to use their gifts to influence the world, improve and empower the lives of others, and bring glory to God in the process.

The Example of Daniel

THE CULTURE AROUND HIM

In the sixth century BC, King Belshazzar threw a wild and extravagant party for a thousand of his friends. While inebriated, the king brought out the golden vessels that had been taken by his predecessor, Nebuchadnezzar, from the temple in Jerusalem. As he, his nobles, his wives, and his concubines drank raucously from the holy temple vessels, they began to praise their man-made gods—their idols.

THE HANDWRITING ON THE WALL

"At that moment the fingers of a man's hand appeared and began writing on the plaster of the king's palace wall next to the lampstand. As the king watched the hand that was writing, his face turned pale, and his thoughts so terrified him that his hip joints shook and his knees knocked together" (Dan. 5:5–6).

Belshazzar was scared to death. He called in all of his wise men to read the handwriting on the wall. The king's perplexity and panic mounted as he realized that none of his wise men could read or interpret the inscription. As a result of the outcry of the crowd, the queen entered the banquet hall and made this pronouncement:

"May the king live forever," she said. "Don't let your thoughts terrify you or your face be pale. There is a man in your kingdom who has the spirit of the holy gods in him. In the days of your predecessor he was found to have insight, intelligence, and wisdom like the wisdom of the gods. Your predecessor, King Nebuchadnezzar, appointed him chief of the diviners, mediums, Chaldeans, and astrologers. Your own predecessor, the king, [did this] because Daniel, the one the king named Belteshazzar, was found to have an extraordinary spirit, knowledge and perception, and the ability to interpret dreams, explain riddles, and solve problems. Therefore, summon Daniel, and he will give the interpretation." (Dan. 5:10–12)

The king did summon Daniel, and Daniel was able to read the handwriting on the wall. The news wasn't good for the king. Because of Belshazzar's arrogant defiance of God, God planned to give his kingdom over to the Medes and the Persians. That same night Belshazzar was killed, and Darius the Mede became king in his stead.

THE QUALITIES OF DANIEL

1. The queen described Daniel as "a man who has the spirit of the holy gods in him." Although this queen reigned in a heathen land, she recognized the power of God in Daniel's life.

2. Daniel was smart. "He was found to have insight, intelligence, and wisdom like the wisdom of the gods."

3. Daniel "was found to have an extraordinary spirit, knowledge and perception, and the ability to interpret dreams, explain riddles, and solve problems." Daniel's intelligence was useful—it helped others. He was able to apply the knowledge he had been given by God to the people around him, as well as to the problems and events that affected their world.

4. Daniel had sterling character. Later we find that as Daniel distinguished himself in King Darius's service, his coworkers became jealous and plotted to discredit him. This story provides us with yet another description of Daniel's character: "The administrators and satraps, therefore, kept trying to find a charge against Daniel regarding the kingdom. But they could find no charge or corruption, for

he was trustworthy, and *no negligence or corruption was found in him*" (Dan. 6:4, author emphasis).

5. Daniel exhibited great courage and faith in the midst of adversity. We all know the story of Daniel's being thrown into the lion's den, and how God shut the mouth of the lions and delivered Daniel. He was a man of great faith who totally trusted in the power and goodness of God.

6. He openly acknowledged God and gave Him the glory for the victories and successes in his life. "Then Daniel spoke with the king: 'May the king live forever. My God sent His angel and shut the lions' mouths'" (Dan. 6:21–22).

THE SECRET BEHIND DANIEL'S SUCCESS

Daniel knew how to say no to temptation. When Babylon conquered Judah, Daniel was pressed into the service of King Nebuchadnezzar. From the beginning, Daniel made up his mind that he "would not defile himself with the king's food or with the wine he drank. So he asked permission from the chief official not to defile himself" (Dan. 1:8).

God blessed Daniel and gave him specific wisdom for the tasks he would be called upon to perform. "God gave these four young men knowledge and understanding in every kind of literature and wisdom. Daniel also understood visions and dreams of every kind" (Dan. 1:17).

Daniel prayed and sought God when he needed help and under-standing. King Nebuchadnezzar had a dream that none of his wise men could interpret, and so the king ordered that all his wise men be killed, including Daniel and his friends. Daniel went to his friends with the matter "[urging] them to ask the God of heaven for mercy concerning this mystery, so Daniel and his friends would not be killed with the rest of Babylon's wise men. The mystery was then revealed to Daniel in a vision at night, and Daniel praised the God of heaven" (Dan. 2:18–19).

While Daniel was both brave and intelligent, he demonstrated respect and discernment in dealing with others. He was humble, not arrogant. When Daniel made up his mind not to eat the king's food or drink the king's wine, he could have simply made a public announcement that he was not participating in this ungodly pro-gram. Instead, the Scripture tells us that he went to the commander of the officials and asked permission of him. When the commander hesitated because he was worried that he might have to pay the price for Daniel's decision, Daniel came up with the idea of having a ten-day trial period for him and his friends. The commander agreed.

Daniel must have also been very levelheaded. When all the wise men in Babylon were panicking because they could not interpret the king's dream and they knew they were facing certain death, Daniel remained calm. Again we read, "Then Daniel responded with tact and discretion to Arioch, the commander of the king's guard, who had gone out to execute the wise men of Babylon" (Dan. 2:14).

I think it is important to remember that Daniel served those around him by helping them: the queen called him a problem solver, and King Darius appointed him as one of three commissioners to be in charge of his entire kingdom. He had to have been a remarkable leader (and problem solver) to qualify for this position.

Following David's Example

The life of Daniel provides an excellent study for us to use to teach the principles of leadership to our children. Daniel loves God and finds himself in a culture hostile to his beliefs. He must resist the temptation to abandon his standards and adopt the worldly standards around him. He is confronted with a series of problems he is called upon to solve. With each new challenge, he seeks God for help, insight, and deliverance. God gives insight and intelligence to Daniel that enables him to solve the problems of the people and, in the process, bring glory to God. Daniel faces adversity and danger with unwavering faith and courage. In every challenge he faces, he trusts God to help him, teach him, strengthen him, and deliver him.

Daniel was a teenager living in Judah when he was taken away to Babylon. He was good-looking, intelligent, and discerning, and appears to have been of noble birth. Daniel was not spoiled by his gifts or position. Apparently Daniel had a well-cultivated root system that was bearing much fruit in his life in Babylon. His life was marked by "faith, prayer, courage, discernment, consistency, and lack of compromise."[1]

These character traits give us a goal to work toward as we raise our children. When they leave home, we want our children, like Daniel, to be prepared for the course God has appointed for them to run. We might argue that we can't do for our children what Daniel's parents did for him—after all, we are not royalty. In a very real sense, we need to consider that our children are in fact royalty: they are sons and daughters of the King of the universe, and we need to raise them accordingly. The character traits that epitomized Daniel are not dependent on money or noble birth. The same God who created Daniel created our children. The same God who equipped Daniel to run his race will equip our children to run their races.

Daniel seems to have possessed a very strong biblical world-view by the time he was taken into captivity. He had strong convictions: he was aware that eating the king's food and drinking his wine would defile him, and he was willing to take a stand for his convictions in a place where he had absolutely no power or clout. Calling on God for wisdom, insight, and help did not seem to be out of the ordinary for him, but rather a learned and practiced response to problems. He also seemed to accept the adversity in his life with faith and without bitterness; adversity seemed to make Daniel stronger.

The Challenge

We want our children to be leaders like Daniel. We want them to be able to draw strength from their roots when they leave home to meet the temptations and challenges of our secular culture. We want observers to recognize the Spirit of God within them as they bring glory to God by using their gifts to solve problems in the world. We want our homes to be effective, intensive leadership training centers.

Leaders by the Grace of God

God has continually surprised me by what He has done in the lives of our children during the twenty-one years we have homeschooled. He has taught them principles from His Word that I never taught them. He has given them opportunities that I never could have arranged. He has opened doors for them, made provision for them, and gifted them in ways that I cannot take credit for.

His greatest surprises, gifts, and provisions have come sometimes in areas where I have been the most worried and fearful. When the boys were young and we spent so much time at the State House working on homeschooling issues, I stayed concerned over the workbooks we left unfinished, certain that I had ruined their educations. What a marvelous gift to look back and realize that God had developed His own leadership training track for Ty and John that included intense hands-on training in civics, government, and politics. They never could have learned from a textbook what they learned from being in the midst of the political pressure cooker as we lobbied together, attended hearings together, stuffed envelopes at two o'clock in the morning, worked on political campaigns, camped out at the State House, and worked to organize the homeschooling grassroots community in South Carolina. They were with me when we won and when we lost, when we cried out to God for help and when we rejoiced in His remarkable interventions. They learned that God does indeed rule in the affairs of men and the affairs of state—and they learned this when they were very young.

Their political training continued as God opened amazing doors for them when they were in high school. Senator Giese, who had sponsored all of our homeschooling legislation, arranged for both boys to serve as pages for him in the South Carolina Senate for several years while they were in high school, although that position is almost always reserved for college students. Then I "inadvertently" found out about the United States Senate Page Program just in time for Ty to apply. Both Ty and John spent six weeks in Washington, D.C., serving as pages for Senator Strom Thurmond.

During Ty's sophomore year in high school, I met Tim Echols, the founder of the TeenPact Program. TeenPact is a one-week, hands-on training course taught for teens by teens at state capitols around the country. Teens hear from legislators, lobbyists, state officials, and others during the course of the week. They take prayer walks, learn how a bill becomes a law, and study campaign disclosure statements. At the time I met Tim, TeenPact classes had never been held outside the state of Georgia. In 1995, Tim brought TeenPact to South Carolina and has every year since. Even with Ty's and John's governmental experience, they benefited greatly from this week, and they both eventually served on TeenPact staffs in other states. John worked as an intern for a portion of his senior year, traveling around the country teaching classes to other teens.

God delights in opening doors for our children. I tell you these things to give you a vision for what can happen in your home. If I thought these experiences were unique to my sons but not available to others, I would never share them with you. These, or similar experiences to these, are available to your students. Make it a point to acquaint your children with local, state, and federal government through field trips and programs like TeenPact. (Don't be afraid to learn right along with your children.) Home School Legal Defense Association has recently launched Generation Joshua, a civics program for homeschoolers that involves online curriculum and hands-on experiences. Patrick Henry College also offers weeklong summer camps for high schoolers that focus on political activism, American history, and similar topics. Your state homeschool organization might also have information on programs in your state for home-schooled students.

Contact information:

Generation Joshua: www.generationjoshua.org
Phone: (540) 338-5600
Patrick Henry College: www.phc.edu
Phone: (540) 338-1776
TeenPact Leadership Schools: www.teenpact.com
Phone: (888) 343-1776
Find your state homeschooling organization:
www.lifeway.com/homeschool

The Leadership Legacy

I do believe that all homeschoolers should be raised to be well-informed, involved citizens. We have a lot at stake and cannot afford to take our freedom for granted or we will lose what we have fought so hard to gain. But we make a mistake when we limit our focus on leadership to the political realm. The goal is for our children to demonstrate leadership in the areas where they are gifted. As you take it upon yourself to study your children and understand their bent, look for ways that your children can develop leadership skills through exercising these strengths.

Don't grow weary in this task of constantly looking for ways to allow your child to impact the world around him with his gifts. This is our ultimate goal—to teach our children to apply what they have learned through the gifts they have been given to solve real problems and help their neighbor. John Maxwell, author and leadership guru, reminds us, "Every effective leadership mentor makes the development of leaders one of his highest priorities in life."[2] As Christian, homeschooling parents, we are truly leadership mentors for our children.

In John Maxwell's book *The 21 Irrefutable Laws of Leadership,* the last chapter is entitled "The Law of Legacy: A Leader's Lasting Value Is Measured by Succession."[3] In this chapter Maxwell makes the point we should "lead with tomorrow as well as today in mind." This reminds me of the diagnostic questions in chapter 4. As our child's leadership coach, we should be constantly asking, "Where does he want to go and how can we get him there?" That is leading with tomorrow in mind. Maxwell also says that we ought to make the process of developing leadership a part of our culture.[4] While he is talking about organizations, I think this is applicable to the family culture as well. We should be faithfully looking for ways to develop our children's potential by enhancing their leadership skills.

Communication and Leadership Go Hand in Hand

It doesn't matter how bright a leader is, how adept he is at solving problems, how gifted he is, or how well he can handle challenges if he cannot effectively communicate his knowledge and ideas to others. We learn many principles of good communication from Daniel. He knew how to be discreet and discerning in his conversation with others. He knew how and when to make an appeal to those in authority, and he knew when to stand firmly on conviction and principle. He was not foolhardy or cowardly in his speech.

Children who grow up in families who communicate well will usually be good communicators. Your children will have an advantage in developing their communication skills since they have observed you work hard at communicating and expressing yourself with them.

Interpersonal communications and public speaking have many skills in common. The one thing that sets them most apart is fear—most people are very fearful of speaking publicly. Encourage your children in small ways when they are young to express themselves before a group: have them stand and recite Bible verses or give book reports to your family, your extended family, or small support group meetings. As they get older and you want to give them some formal training, I would recommend Dr. Jeff Myer's material to you, especially his *Secrets of Great Communicators* series. You can find this on his Web site at www.myersinstitute.com. Older students who are interested in further training can profit greatly from involvement in speech and debate. Most state home-schooling organizations can put you in touch with speech and debate teams in your state.

In communication, both the spoken and the written word have tremendous significance. To find a writing curriculum that is appropriate for your child's age and learning style, I would once again recommend Cathy Duffy's *100 Top Picks for Homeschool Curriculum.* In the chapter on language arts curriculum, she features curriculum for both composition and speech.

Jesus is the Ultimate Communicator. He has communicated to us in word and in deed exactly who God is and what He expects from us. He is the Word Incarnate. Language is His gift to us. We need to work diligently at turning our homes into environments bursting with language. Then our children, like Daniel, will be able to use language in an appealing way to bring glory to God in our culture.

Who Will Read the Handwriting on the Wall Today?

Like Belshazzar of old, today's world faces problems that cause even the strongest person to turn pale and knock at the knees. My hope is that this generation of homeschooled children will become the Daniels of their world: young men and women who are zealously jealous for God's honor; young adults known for their wisdom and intelligence, who can explain riddles and solve difficult problems by applying biblical principles to the perplexities at hand; people the world recognizes as having a spirit, a power, and an intelligence that must come from God—even though the world does not know God.

Our children are truly God's gift to us and our gift to a needy world. Don't grow weary or lose heart in this tremendous opportunity you have of raising up a new generation of Daniels to bring God's power and grace to bear on the problems and needs of this world. As you work hard at cultivating your children's potential, remember that they, in turn, will be uniquely prepared to impact their culture for Christ. May our children exclaim to the world by their words and their lives, "To God be the glory!"

epilogue

today all three of my children were home for lunch. It was like old times. We sat around the table, laughing and talking, while we watched the press conference announcing that Steve Spurrier will be the new football coach for the University of South Carolina. Everyone had opinions to share on Spurrier (the new coach), Lou Holtz (the former coach), and the big fight at the Carolina/Clemson football game last Saturday. That prompted a round of discussion on violence and behavior that somehow sparked a round of discussion on hunting licenses, which somehow led to a conversation about a Bible study that John and Lizzy are attending together at USC.

Conversations like these are the stuff life is made of—the insignificant, the funny, the eternal—somehow blending seamlessly together during the course of a normal meal. All three children are grown now. Ty is twenty-six and is working in a very demanding sales job. John is twenty-four and preparing for the LSAT, trying to discern if God is calling him to law school next year (not dental school after all). Lizzy is finishing high school and is in the midst of making the "college decision." She is seriously considering a couple of small Christian schools six to eight hours from home.

I looked at them today and wondered where the time has gone. It seems like just yesterday that they were fourteen, twelve, and five, and we were eating lunch together everyday. I was still the chief teacher, cook, chauffeur, events coordinator, counselor, and resident cheerleader. Those were exhausting and exhilarating days, and I miss them (although twelve years ago, I probably thought they were more exhausting than exhilarating!).

Next year, for the first time in twenty-seven years, Joe and I will be home alone. After twenty-one years, my homeschooling career will be completed. I can't believe how quickly the time has flown. It seems like yesterday I was moaning because I thought I would have a child in diapers forever. As our children leave home, our nest might be empty from time to time, but our hearts are gloriously full of thanksgiving for what God has done. I look at my three children, and I know that they are gifts from God. I am so thankful for each of them, and the privilege of being their mother. I thank God for every day I had with them—for the laughter, the tears, the arguments, the times of prayer, the crises, the joys, the successes, and the work.

I am especially thankful God led us to homeschool. I am thankful for the strength of our relationships, the time we have had together, and the very eventful journey we have taken together along the way. I am also very thankful that they each love God and trust Him daily to lead them. I am deeply grateful for Joe and the strong marriage we share. Together we are excited about Ty, John, Lizzy, their future spouses, and our future grandchildren.

Most of all, I rejoice to know that it doesn't end here. Heaven is on the horizon. How glorious to know that in eternity Joe and I will once again have unlimited time with our children—and their children and their children.

You may still be in the throes of everyday life, overworked and stressed with the constant demands of children. You may be anticipating beginning your own family. Wherever you are in the course of your family life, I hope you will take a few minutes now to stop and reflect on that point in time when your children, like mine, will be leaving home. Think now about your goals for your children and home life, and what you want to accomplish, as well as what you want them to accomplish between now and then.

I pray that as you have read this book, you have been encouraged in your call to cultivate a rich harvest for God's glory in the lives of your children. I pray that you feel invigorated and renewed as you consider how best to help your children complete the race God has set before them.

I pray that the winds of the Spirit will blow in your heart, stirring the waters of your soul, and that as you have read this book, He has called you to a new level of insight and conviction concerning the absolute importance of your work in the home. I firmly believe that revival can begin in your home and in my home—in our lives and the lives of our children—if we are willing to hear and heed His call to lay down our lives for those He has put in our care.

Eternity hangs in the balance.

From Ty, age 26 . . .

Homeschooling has uniquely prepared me for life, has taught me to deal with the constant decisions that confront me in the business world, and has equipped me to face whatever the world throws my way. I would like to address the main questions that people ask me about homeschooling in hopes of offering encouragement to those of you who feel called to homeschool your children but are questioning the validity of that call.

The first question people always ask is, "What about socialization?" To be completely honest, when people ask me that question, I just have to laugh. When I was in the ninth grade, my grandfather took my cousin Mary, an eleventh grader, and me to her high school football game. His doubts about socialization dissipated when, throughout the course of the game, he saw me introducing my cousin to students from *her* school and the other high school. My world was not confined to one particular school. I was able to make and cultivate friendships with students from all the schools in the area. Neither was my social arena confined to one generation— I was at the game with my granddad.

In 1996, I was afforded the privilege of being a page for Senator Strom Thurmond in the United States Senate. Two fellow pages constantly gave me a hard time about homeschooling and socialization. We were in the mailroom one day sorting Senator Thurmond's mail when this discussion once again occurred. We walked back into the lobby of the Senator's office at the same time his one o'clock appointment arrived. I heard a man say, "Ty! What are you doing here?!" I looked up and saw Senator Ryberg, a South Carolina state senator, and Mr. Burgess, from the State Budget and Control Board. I introduced Senator Ryberg and Mr. Burgess to the employees in the office. Situations like this happened continually during my stint as a page. Fellow pages stopped wondering about my socialization and no longer gave me a hard time for being homeschooled; in fact, before our tenure as pages was over, they both told me that they had held misconceptions about homeschooling.

Through homeschooling I was surrounded by and interacted with people from different generations, so, for me, there never was a generation gap. I was also able to be involved in various extra-curricular activities and pursued what I loved: sports and the out-doors. The world was my classroom, and every day I was free to explore my classroom and become a hands-on learner. Mom knew my learning style and knew exactly how to present various subjects in ways that I could understand, and in ways that would stick.

Instead of reading out of a book about parliamentary procedure and state government, Mom took me to the State House and taught me about it there. Instead of reading to me about the armed forces, she took me to Fort Jackson and let me watch the soldiers train and taught me about it there. Instead of reading to me about the importance of taking care of those less fortunate, every Christmas she signed us up to work with Project Angel Tree to volunteer time and to adopt a family. We are all called to be doers of the Word, not just hearers, and we are called to take action. Through homeschooling,

Mom taught me how to be a doer of the Word, not just a hearer, and how to take action. I could learn and enjoy life without constantly having to worry about what my peers would think.

Homeschooling prepared me to be an active participant in God's kingdom and allowed me to grow and develop in conjunction with the way God created me. I was not forced into a learning program that was good for the majority, but not for me, and my educational path was not placed under the care of someone who did not have a vested interest in my life. Instead, I received an education tailored for me, taught by the person who had the most vested interest in my life: my mom.

During the fall of 1999, for the first time in my life, I had to say to myself, "I just can't do it." I was curled up on the couch in my college dorm room, discouraged, hurt, tired, 350 miles away from home and faced with a harsh reality. Two months prior, I lost the vision in my right eye, and for the first time in my life I was physically unable to do something. Through my parents' guidance and teaching growing up, I knew that I could do anything I set my sights on. But on this December day, I realized that I would no longer be able to play college soccer, or play in any competitive league ever again. As a member of the Covenant College soccer team, I had to address the team and give them my farewell as a teammate. That was the hardest "speech" I have ever given. My life was dedicated to soccer; I lived and breathed it, but now I had to say good-bye to a sport that captured my life. I had to say, "I just can't do it." What a blessing it was that I went twenty-one years without ever saying, "I can't do it." Because of Mom and Dad's dedication to my well-being and their encouragement in all of my endeavors, I never said, "I can't." (My sight miraculously came back a year-and-a-half later, but that's another story.)

What Satan means for evil, God means for good. Romans 8:28 reads, "In all things God works for the good of those who love him" (NIV). God closed that door so He could work in my life and have 100 percent of my attention. I transferred to the University of South Carolina and lived at home for the remainder of my college career. For the first time I was living at home but going to school away from home. I was able to watch Mom balance her job (her writing) and teaching Lizzy; and as a grownup I could see all the sacrifices she made for me all along.

Maybe you have been wrestling with the idea of homeschooling but are worried about the social and logistical ramifications. "Do not fear, for I am with you; do not be dismayed, for I am your God. I will strengthen you and help you; I will uphold you with my righteous right hand" (Isa. 41:10 NIV). So I encourage you now, do not worry yourself out of the biggest blessing you can give your kids and your family. Do not be dismayed by our society, because the blessing that you and your family will receive far outweighs the flack from others. When you choose to homeschool, you choose to give what you know to be best to your children. God will honor that decision and will give you the strength you need along the way.

I know that every mother wants the absolute best for her children, and that many like the idea of homeschooling but do not think they have what it takes. I will be the first to tell you that my mom is an extraordinary woman, and God has blessed her in her endeavors. But there were times along the way that she wondered if what she was doing was right. Hardships will come and doubts will arise. Do not give up and do not give in. God has blessed you with children and will enable you to make the best decisions for them while they are in your care.

Mom, thank you for making this decision for me when I was six, and for seeing it through to fruition. I love you and look forward to passing this blessing on to my family in the years to come.

From John, age 24 . . .

My greatest memories of homeschooling center around the enjoyment we shared as a family. We loved being together and learning together.

In the traditional method of schooling, to the young boy, fun seems outlawed. The boy's imagination is confined to a classroom, shackled to a desk with the key thrown out until compulsory attendance is satisfied. Thankfully, as a young boy, my classroom and desk were not limited to a stationary position. Rather than merely reading a textbook, taking a test, and receiving some quantitative mark suggesting the level of my intelligence, we had discussions and went on family vacation field trips. Education is qualitative, not just quantitative. The quality of education that Ty, Liz, and I received was in no way sterile. It was meaningful and enjoyable. Historic Williamsburg, Cape Canaveral, many state and national parks, and various museums; Washington, D.C., the South Carolina legislature, and numerous state capitols; church, grocery stores, shops, home, the outdoors, the indoors: these were my classrooms and my playground. The joy of learning was always a thread in our homeschool.

I will never forget being four years old, marching behind Mom and Ty, beating a Fisher Price plastic drum, waving an American flag, and singing "You're a Grand Ol' Flag" at the top of my lungs with chubby, rosy cheeks. I can recall laughing my head off because of Dad reading parts in *Julius Caesar* by Shakespeare in funny, cultural accents. Going to the Veterans' Day Parade dressed in every piece of camouflage that I owned while carrying a toy gun was a treat. Growing up, I didn't know that school was supposed to be boring.

It was not just the subject material that made our schooling exciting. It is not merely the fact that we are all fun-loving individuals that made it great. God has blessed us with a love for and enjoyment of each other. I never doubted the fact that Mom and Dad enjoy being around their children. I have always known that Ty and Liz are two of the best friends I will have. Sure, we had our share of fights, arguments, disagreements, headlocks, and unofficial wrestling matches to determine who was right, but we love each other and enjoy being together.

Many theologians argue that the chief end of man is "to glorify God and enjoy Him forever." Part of glorifying God is having fun with the family that He has blessed one with. Even when jobs were lost, someone was very sick or injured, or when Mom was writing a book, God has called us to enjoy being together. When I consider my parents, the many sacrifices that they have made for me and the selfless love which they continually express toward me, I am much more touched by the fact that they enjoy being with me.

Zephaniah 3:17 says:

> The LORD your God is with you,
>> he is mighty to save.
> He will take great delight in you,
>> he will quiet you with his love,
>> he will rejoice over you with singing. (NIV)

Our Lord enjoys being with us. According to Scripture, He rejoices over us with singing. He desires to be with us so much that He sacrificed His son and raised him up that we may be co-heirs with Christ. In His selfless love, Christ has called us righteous and blessed us with His Spirit. All because God enjoys being with us.

May God bless you with a family that enjoys being together. Homeschooling does not guarantee this. Rather, it is a tool that the Lord uses to help bring this about. Sing in your house, take field trips, go on vacations, have fun together.

From Lizzy, age 17 . . .

God has given me many blessings—salvation, most importantly, as well as a loving church and reliable, trustworthy friends. But one of the most meaningful blessings in my life is homeschooling. I've been homeschooled since kindergarten (I'm now a senior in high school), and it has been a life-changing experience. I love it!

One aspect of homeschooling that I greatly appreciate is what it's brought to my social life. I am reminded of people's negative stereotypes of homeschoolers regularly by the question, "Do you have any friends?" Homeschooling has given me freedom from having a set group of friends determined by age and grade within the confines of a classroom. This freedom enables me to have friends of all ages who are not only fun to be with, but who encourage me in my walk with Christ.

In many ways I'm a typical teenage girl. I enjoy shopping, being with my friends, and going to Starbucks. I've been to proms (at a Christian school), and sometimes I talk on my cell phone too much. Society wants to destroy girls' worth by telling them their importance is derived from popularity, beauty, and success, but I know God has created me for so much more. Even as a "sheltered" homeschooler, the pressure I feel as a teenage girl is heavy—buy certain clothes, be smart, be pretty, be talented, and always have lots of friends and at least one boyfriend. But none of those things have ever mattered to me because I know that my relationship with God is infinitely more important. Homeschooling is one of the primary tools my parents have used to instill that truth in me.

Because my education is Christ-focused, I have gained a sense of self-worth that keeps me from looking for security in friends. I've seen many Christians waste the important formative years of adolescence trying to "fit in." They deny who God created them to be by changing to please their friends. I've never resorted to that behavior because Mom and Dad have taught me that I am created in the image of God.

As a result of the deep love my parents show me, I never go looking for affirmation from other relationships. I am free to be myself and enjoy my friends, but not let them determine who I am. I now realize the confidence of identity I have isn't magic, but a result of my parents' hard work. Mom structured my education to constantly remind me of God's omnipotence in creating all things. She engraved absolute truth into my mind through extensive worldview training. Through my one-on-one education, she developed the gifts and talents God gave me so they can be utilized to impact the culture for Christ.

One of the biggest benefits of my homeschooling experience is the closeness it's given me to my brothers. Even though we weren't sitting next to each other every minute we were doing schoolwork, we were still together. My two brothers and I have a relationship unlike most siblings because of the quality time we've spent together. Most people my age think it's weird, but I consider them to be my two best friends. I confide in them about everything. Those bonds we developed during homeschooling didn't diminish with age, but have grown: I talk to my brothers several times a week (they're grown now), and we are very involved in each others' lives. Anytime I'm in a performance or a competition, they're on the front row cheering me on.

One thing I hear a lot from people who are thinking about homeschooling is, "I could never do that because my mom, my brother/sister, and I would fight all the time." What a sad thought, that the more time you spend together the worse your relationship gets. In our homeschooling, we helped each other through math problems and rejoiced when someone did well on a test. Because you're working closely together, it gives an irreplaceable bond that will carry into the rest of your lives.

In closing, I have one message to send to homeschooling mothers: *keep on doing what you're doing.* Looking back on my home-schooling years, I wouldn't trade them for the world. The opportunities it gave me, the education I received, and the irreplaceable relationships with my brothers and parents are precious gifts. I know it gets tough, but one day your kids will have the same message for you that I have for my mom: *Thanks, Mom, I'm going to miss this.*

appendix

my homeschooling journey

The First Battle: A Personal One

In 1984, Joe and I were faced with choosing between public and Christian school for our oldest son, Ty, who was then turning six. Even as a child he was bright, gregarious, energetic, and challenging. His kindergarten experience should have been delightful. He was attending a church school. His class consisted of a creative teacher and eight children. They were beginning reading, and by February, Ty was the only child not reading well. I watched as his extroverted personality began the metamorphosis into introversion. I knew I had to do something to rescue my child; I just didn't know what. I pulled him out of school in February with the intention of holding him back a year and allowing him to repeat K-5, enabling him to be at his prime, rather than behind, when he began first grade. Within weeks, his vitality and love of life returned. I had my son back.

I prayed and agonized over where to put Ty in school. We were at a crossroads in his little life, and I felt like I was faced with a lose-lose situation. At that point in time, our church school was using a curriculum with little use for the concept of readiness. I knew if Ty were exposed to a grueling year of academics, it could be his undoing. The public school seemed to have a better grasp of what five-year-olds needed, but could not share or affirm our Christian worldview. In the Christian school, his worldview would remain intact, while his confidence and joy would be crushed by academic pressure for which he was not ready.

In the midst of this agonizing process, I poured out my heart to a dear friend as we got together for our weekly time of prayer and Bible study. As I laid before Susan my choices for Ty and asked her to pray for Joe and me, she very quietly told me of her intention to homeschool her son. I will never forget the first time I heard that word, *homeschool.* The walls of Susan's little mobile home (she and her husband were seminary students preparing for the mission field) began to close in on me. My head was spinning, and I felt trapped. I graciously took the literature Susan offered me and ran out the door. I knew I would never homeschool.

Along with some short studies, Susan gave me a copy of Dr. Raymond Moore's *Home Grown Kids.* Very reluctantly, I picked up the book and began to read. In spite of wanting to totally dismiss the idea of home education from my mind, I found myself increasingly fascinated by the principles espoused by Dr. and Mrs. Moore. Now I was truly in a quandary. I wanted to narrow my options for Ty, but found the field broadened instead to three choices—public, private, and home.

When the boys were young, I used my early morning walks as a time to clear my mind, meditate on Scripture, and pray. During one of those walks, I came to grips with what I had been denying for weeks: God was leading me to homeschool Ty. To appreciate the anguish I was in, you must remember that I knew no one—not one person in the entire world—who was actually homeschooling. *Homeschooling* was not a household word as it is today. As I walked, I told the Lord that I was sorry, but I just couldn't homeschool. To this day I can remember the sound of a large metal door slamming shut in my mind, and God saying to me, "Oh, yes, you will."

When I returned home from my walk, I immediately contacted the local public school district to find out how to enroll Ty as a K-5 student for the coming school year. By ten o'clock that morning, I had met with the appropriate school officials who completed Ty's enrollment in a matter of minutes. The sense of relief was overwhelming. The monkey was off my back, and I could finally get some rest. I continued to tell myself how ridiculous I had been to consider something like homeschooling.

From March until May of 1984, my life was incredibly peaceful—until all the other parents of K-5 students in our neighborhood received a packet of information from the public school about kindergarten orientation. When I called the principal to find out why we had not received a packet, he curtly informed me that I could not put my six-year-old in his K-5 program. Ty would have to enter school in the first grade. I calmly explained that his staff had guaranteed Ty a place in kindergarten, to no avail.

I was still not extremely concerned because I had several acquaintances in the district office, and I knew them to be reasonable people. When I called and explained my predicament to an associate superintendent, I could tell I had reached an impasse. I used what I considered my trump card by threatening to home-school Ty if I could not hold him back (as the school had already agreed to do). I knew no school administrator would encourage homeschooling if he could help it. To my amazement and horror, the superintendent informed me the school board had become lenient with that type of thing. I later learned they had approved one homeschool program in the history of the district, and that mother had been a certified teacher. I had graduated from college with an economics degree.

Joe and I quickly realized we were going to have to hire an attorney. Just finding a lawyer who had ever heard of homeschooling was difficult. Finding one who understood homeschooling in the context of school law and constitutional rights seemed impossible. Additionally, we were a young family, with limited financial resources. By God's grace, we found a Christian attorney who cut his fees and took our case.

Our attorney's first task was to research what we had to do to comply with South Carolina law, as both the local school district and the State Department of Education refused to provide us with that information. There were of course no support groups or state organizations to call on for information, advice, or support. We submitted our application in July 1984. Even though we had carefully complied with the law, the school board denied our application because I was not a certified teacher (which was not a requirement of the law). When I opened the letter of rejection from the school board, I felt physically ill. Private schools were filled by this point in the summer, the school district would not allow me to hold Ty back, and now they denied my request to homeschool. What was I to do? We once again hired our attorney to file the proper paperwork for us to appeal our case to the State Board of Education, as well as represent us there.

Our prospects looked bleak. We were informed by several officials that the State Board of Education, in cases like ours, simply upheld the local school board's decision. The mounting legal and financial implications invaded our lives as we suddenly faced the possibility of expensive appeals, coupled with the frightening prospect of having our children forcibly removed from our home. I will never forget those feelings of fear and panic as long as I live.

In the midst of our dilemma, I decided to visit the State Superintendent of Education in South Carolina and explain our quandary to him. (I felt comfortable doing this because I had known him since I was a child. He had chosen to observe my mother's public school classroom for a period of months while working on his Ph.D. in education.) With our state board hearing just a week away, the superintendent threatened to put me in jail for truancy. I left the State Department reeling. Not only had I not wanted to homeschool, now I was going to be put in jail for it. This nightmare was careening totally out of control.

No family members knew of our plans to homeschool at this point except my sister. With this new threat of jail, I had no choice but to tell my parents. I was slightly hysterical when I broke the news to them—beginning with homeschooling and ending with jail. They had never heard of homeschooling before either, but my father was furious with the way I had been treated. As a teacher, Mom was focused on the educational aspect of things, knowing how wonderful it would be to teach one on one on a daily basis. Even though I know they had to have misgivings (I had misgivings), they were never anything but supportive of our decision to homeschool.

The day after my homeschool confession, Dad, in his capacity as chairman of the board at Baptist Medical Center, Columbia, was speaking at a meeting with Nancy Thurmond, wife of U. S. Senator Strom Thurmond. He informed her of my dilemma and told her that I had contacted the senator's office, to no avail. (I had worked for Senator Thurmond for a short stint when I was in high school.) Dad wanted to know then what the senator planned to do to help me. Mrs. Thurmond called the senator in Washington, D.C., and a few days later he flew to Columbia, met personally with the State

Superintendent of Education, and "asked" him to approve my home-schooling program. Needless to say, my program was approved, and I never went to jail.[1]

The Second Battle: State and National Ramifications

Rather than being the end of our story, this was just the beginning. The Lord, in His sovereignty, had allowed me to experience those feelings of panic and fear for a reason. Now I had a burden to help homeschooling families facing the same intimidation and prejudice. I had no idea at the time that the next phase of the journey would span eight years and would be a perilous uphill climb, involving all sorts of legislative and legal maneuverings.

In December 1985, a neighbor informed me of regulations promulgated by the state department of education requiring home-schooling parents to possess a college degree from an accredited institution, and to use only state-approved texts in their home-schools. This negated the use of Christian curricula in homeschools.

Once again I called our attorney and explained our predicament. He coached me through the process of calling for a public hearing on the regulations and bringing in expert testimony to rebut them. Joe and I received the required sixty-day notification from the state board about the hearing date (to be held in May 1986) the same day I lost a little baby girl between the fifth and sixth month of my pregnancy. I almost lost my life as well during the labor and delivery process. Years later when I found our planning notes for the meeting, they were tear-stained. Because of the severe time constraints, Joe and I were forced to work on the public hearing in my hospital room after the birth and death of Joy.

Just organizing our side of the public hearing was time consuming, expensive, and emotionally exhausting. We had to pay legal fees and fees associated with the expert witness. After an associate superintendent informed me we would have about twenty-five minutes to present all of our testimony, my father had to get involved to insure that we had adequate time to present our case. Even though we had more than four hundred people and an expert witness in attendance at the hearing, the State Board of Education sent the regulations to the General Assembly for final approval without making any changes in light of the testimony offered.

That summer of 1986, I met with State Senator Warren Giese for the first time. Senator Giese sponsored most of our homeschooling legislation from that point on. As a former USC football coach and a Ph.D. in education, he was well-respected by everyone. He listened to my story and immediately agreed to call a Senate Education Committee hearing on those regulations. We had another huge turnout, and this time the Senate Education Committee unanimously rejected the regulations.

Representative David Beasley encouraged me to work on proactive homeschooling legislation, which we did. The Senate Education Committee called for an ad hoc committee to draft compromise legislation designed to keep homeschoolers and educators happy.

This bill was enacted in June 1988 after the bill was substantially amended. The most onerous provision of the new law was a requirement that teaching parents without a college degree make a passing score on the Education Entrance Examination (the Triple E), a test developed by the state of South Carolina to screen prospective professional teachers. Mike Farris, president of Home School Legal Defense Association (HSLDA)[2], said this about the law: "Homeschoolers in South Carolina need to be banded together for future action on all fronts. You are saddled with one of the most cumbersome laws in the country. Of all states, you all need to stick together."[3]

Help for the Battle Weary

At this point, HSLDA jumped into the judicial and legislative arenas in South Carolina with both feet, giving us the expertise and support we needed to effectively fight for our freedom. Mike Farris began by filing a class-action suit to overturn the Triple E requirement for homeschool parents. At one point in time, there were more homeschooling lawsuits filed in South Carolina than the other forty-nine states combined.

During this period of intense litigation, one of the attorneys for the State Department of Education said to me, "Zan, I usually say 'Boo!' and groups like yours scatter like scared mice. You not only have legal representation—you have good legal representation. That gives you staying power." When the state ran out of money and had to cease taking depositions, a department of education staffer observed, "HSLDA is like the Energizer bunny™—they keep going and going and going."

Amidst the appeals process for the Triple E case, I began researching the feasibility of forming a private organization to serve as an alternative to public school supervision for homeschooling parents. In July 1990, the South Carolina Association of Independent Home Schools (SCAIHS)[4] was incorporated. Wanting to prepare for any type of legal challenge, we required all SCAIHS members to be HSLDA members too. Only three months later, a school district filed truancy charges against eleven SCAIHS families. Additionally, the state attorney general issued an opinion that SCAIHS was not a legally valid option for homeschool families. Emboldened by this opinion, other districts began filing charges against homeschooling families. HSLDA countered by filing a class-action suit on behalf of SCAIHS members, asserting that SCAIHS was in fact a legal option for homeschoolers.

South Carolina homeschoolers were fighting a war on two fronts—one against the Triple E legislation and one in support of SCAIHS.

Victory!

After battling the Triple E case through the South Carolina court system, HSLDA won a landmark victory in the State Supreme Court in December 1991. Many other states had been waiting in the wings with plans to test nondegreed parents before granting them approval to homeschool. HSLDA's victory nipped this dangerous trend in the bud.

The decision also paved the way for us to work on the passage of a bill that would make SCAIHS a legal option for homeschooling families, negating the need for them to go through their local school boards. Senator Giese, my father, Dr. Steve Suits, Dr. Jim Carper, John Watson, and I[5] formed a legislative committee and, along with the SCAIHS staff and members, worked relentlessly for four months on this bill. We all watched a miracle unfold as the South Carolina General Assembly passed the SCAIHS law in April 1992, ending eight years of legal and legislative turmoil in our state.

Legislative work is never finished, as threats to freedom are always just a bill away. But the hardest part of the work was finished when the State Supreme Court ruled against the Triple E, and the South Carolina General Assembly passed the SCAIHS legislation. Since that time, God has continued to bless homeschooling, and it has continued to grow and prosper in South Carolina. Mothers can now homeschool their children with support and encouragement and without hostility and legal problems.

I served as the president of SCAIHS from 1990 to 2000. Today I am the Homeschool Resource & Media Consultant for Broadman & Holman Publishers, as well as the homeschool editor for Lifeway.com's Web network (www.lifeway.com/homeschool). Now that my children are grown, my desire is to encourage women in the vital kingdom work of raising their children for Christ. I pray this book has been helpful to the end. To God be the glory.

notes

Introduction

1. National Women's History Project Web site. This information was obtained from the "Biography Center," www.nwhp.org/tlp/biographies/steinem/steinem_bio.html.

2. Elizabeth Elliot, *Let Me Be a Woman* (Wheaton, Ill.: Tyndale House Publishers, Inc., 1976), back cover.

3. James G. Small, "I've Found a Friend," *Trinity Hymnal* (1961): 433. The hymn itself was written in 1866.

Chapter 1

1. Elliot, *Let Me Be a Woman,* 65.

2. Ibid., 67.

Chapter 2

1. Merriam-Webster online at www.m-w.com.

2. John Taylor Gatto, *A Different Kind of Teacher* (Berkeley, Calif: Berkeley Hill Books, 2001), 15.

3. C. S. Wyatt. (5 August 2004). Web site: Existentialism: An Introduction, "Camus" [Online]. Available at www.tameri.com/csw/exist.

4. Jay Kessler, quoted in Weldon M. Hardenbrook, *Missing from Action: Vanishing Manhood in America* (Nashville, Tenn.: Thomas Nelson Publishers, 1987), 38–39.

5. Gary DeMar, *God and Government, Vol. 1* (Atlanta: American Vision Press, 1982), 8.

6. Ibid.

7. "Jennifer Roback Morse," Web site for Hoover Institution at Stanford University, www-hoover.stanford.edu/BIOS/morse.html.

8. Jennifer Roback Morse, *Love and Economics: Why the Laissez-Faire Family Doesn't Work* (Dallas, Tx.: Spence Publishing Company, 2001), 3.

9. Personal notes taken from a one-week class taught by Elisabeth Elliot at Columbia Bible College in 1985.

Chapter 3

1. Oprah Winfrey, "Oprah Talks to Jane Fonda," *O: The Oprah Magazine*, July/August 2000, 171.

2. Ibid., 261–262.

3. *Webster's Third New International Dictionary, Unabridged.* Merrian-Webster, 2002, (19 October 2004), http://unabridged.merriam-webster.com.

4. Terry Dorian, Ph.D. and Zan Peters Tyler, *Anyone Can Homeschool* (Lafayette, LA: Huntington House Publishers, 1996), 32.

5. IBid.

6. Charles Spurgeon, *Grace and Power* (New Kensington, Pa.: Whitaker House, 2000), 97.

7. Francis A. Schaeffer, *The God Who Is There* (Downers Grove, Ill.: InterVarsity Press, 1998).

8. Jane M. Healy, Ph.D., *Endangered Minds: Why Our Children Don't Think* (New York, N.Y.: Simon and Schuster, 1990), 88.

9. Ibid., 95.

10. Ibid., 88.

11. Ibid., 91.

12. Ibid., 102. The term *linguistically malnourished* comes from Dr. Healy's book, not the idea that Christian homes should be the protectors and propagators of language in our society.

13. Ibid., 131.

Chapter 4

1. Vivian Doublestein founded the Master's Academy of Fine Arts in September 1990. For more information on the Master's Academy of Fine Arts, visit them online at www.mafa.net.

2. For more information on Excelsior! Academy, visit them online at www.excelsioracademy.org.

3. Charles R. Swindoll, *Growing Wise in Family Life: Bible Study Guide* (Plano, Tx.: Insight for Living, 1988), 36.

4. "Curriculum," *Webster's Third New International Dictionary, Unabridged.* Merriam-Webster, 2002, (4 November 2004), http://unabridged. merriam-webster.com.

5. Personal notes taken from a lecture by Elizabeth Youmens at the Foundations of American Christian Education Apprenticeship Program held in Virginia Beach, Virginia, in June 1998.

6. Swindoll, *Growing Wise in Family Life,* 95.

7. Ted Tripp, *Shepherding a Child's Heart* (Wapwallopen, Pa.: Shepherd Press, 1995), 66–67.

8. For more information on SCAIHS, visit their Web site at www.scaihs.org or call the office at 803-454-0427. The Appendix also has some information on SCAIHS.

9. Gary Chapman and Ross Campbell, *The Five Love Languages of Children* (Chicago, Ill.: Moody Publishers, 1997), 17.

10. Ibid., 17–18.

11. *The Holman Bible Dictionary,* "spiritual gifts," http://bible.life way.com/crossmain.asp.

12. Ibid.

13. "Personality," *Webster's Third New International Dictionary, Unabridged.* Merriam-Webster, 2002, (9 November 2004), http://unabridged.merr iam-webster.com.

14. John Trent, Rick Osborne, and Kurt Bruner, *Parents' Guide to the Spiritual Growth of Children* (Wheaton, Ill.: Tyndale House Publishers, 2000), 91–94.

15. Ibid, 89.

16. Ibid.

17. Ibid.

18. Ibid.

19. Ibid, 87–95.

20. You can find this information online at www.DiscProfile.com.

21. Walter B. Barbe, Ph.D., *Growing Up Learning: The Key to Your Child's Potential* (Washington D.C.: Acropolis Books, Ltd., 1985).

22. Ibid., 11.

23. Ibid., 53.

24. Ibid., 101.

25. Ibid., 49.

26. Cathy Duffy, *100 Top Picks for Homeschool Curriculum* (Nashville, Tenn.: Broadman and Holman Publishers, 2005), chapter 4.

27. This book is available at www.lifeway.com/homeschool.

28. Barbe, *Growing Up Learning,* 15.

29. Isaac Watts, "Jesus Shall Reign Where'er the Sun," *Trinity Hymnal* (1961): 374. The hymn itself was written in 1719.

Chapter 5

1. J. Budziszewski, "The Roots of Law," *Religion & Liberty*, (September/October 2001), Vol. 11, Num. 5; Found on http://www.action.org/publicat/randl/article.php?id=397.

2. Charles Colson and Nancy Pearcey, *How Now Shall We Live?* (Wheaton, Ill.: Tyndale House Publishers, Inc., 1999), 14.

3. David Noebel with Chuck Edwards, *Thinking Like a Christian: Understanding and Living a Biblical Worldview* (Nashville, Tenn.: Broadman & Holman Publishers, 2002), 6.

4. Christopher Catherwood, *Five Leading Reformers* (Great Britain: Christian Focus Publications, 2000), 44.

5. Ibid.

6. Colson and Pearcey, *How Now Shall We Live?,* 294.

7. Ibid., x.

8. Ibid., xi.

9. Alistair McGrath, "Calvin and the Christian Calling," *First Things* 94 (June/July 1999). 31–35.

10. Ibid.

11. Ibid.

12. Colson and Pearcey, *How Now Shall We Live?,* 388.

13. Ibid., 383.

14. Jon Walker, "Family Life Council Says It's Time to Bring Family Back to Life," (12 June 2002), found online at www.sbcannualmeeting.net/sbc02/newsroom/newspage.asp?ID=261.

15. Discussion of these dismal statistics is woven throughout the two worldview books (courses) written by Dr. David Noebel and Chuck Edwards: *Thinking Like a Christian* and *Countering Culture,* published by Broadman & Holman, 2002 and 2004 respectively.

16. Colson and Pearcey, *How Now Shall We Live?,* 384.

17. Noebel, *Thinking Like a Christian,* 158.

18. Christopher Klicka, *Home Schooling: The Right Choice* (Nashville, Tenn.: Broadman & Holman Publishers, 2000), 82.

19. Brian Ray, *2005–2006 Worldwide Guide to Homeschooling: Facts and Stats on the Benefits of Homeschooling* (Nashville, Tenn.: Broadman & Holman Publishers, 2005). Order the book online at www.lifeway.com/homeschool.

20. J. Budziszewski, "Overcoming the Scandal of the Christian Mind," *First Things* 100 (February 2000): 52–56. Found online at www.firstthings.com/ftissues/ft0002/reviews/budziszewski.html. This article is actually a book review of Charles Colson's *How Now Shall We Live?*

21. Ibid.

22. Ellen Ward Gardner, *Life in a New World* (Life in America Publishers, 2001), 256.

23. William J. Federer, *America's God and Country* (Coppell, Tex.: FAME Publishing, Inc., 1996), 700.

24. Ibid., 289.

25. Gary DeMar, *America's Christian Heritage* (Nashville, Tenn.: Broadman & Holman Publishers, 2004), 44.

26. Noebel, *Thinking Like a Christian,* 91.

27. You can find more information about Summit Ministries at www.sum mit.org.

28. You can find more information about Patrick Henry College and their programs at www.phc.edu.

29. You can visit Worldview Academy online at www.worldview.org.

30. David Noebel and Chuck Edwards, *Countering Culture: Arming Yourself to Confront Non-Biblical Worldviews* (Nashville, Tenn.: Broadman & Holman Publishers, 2004), 157.

Chapter 6

1. Walter Bauer, *A Greek-English Lexicon of the New Testament and Other Early Christian Literature,* revised and edited by Frederick William Danker, 3rd ed. (University of Chicago Press, 2000), 609.

2. Oswald Chambers, "All Noble Things Are Difficult, July 7" *My Utmost for His Highest,* found online as part of the Lifeway.com Bible Search Tools, under the category of devotionals.

3. Patricia Hersch, *A Tribe Apart: A Journey into the Heart of American Adolescence* (New York, N.Y.: The Ballantine Publishing Group, 1998), 12.

4. Ibid.

5. Ibid., 11, 30.

6. Ibid., 99.

7. Ibig., 12.

8. Ibid.

9. Glenn T. Stanton, *My Crazy Imperfect Christian Family* (Colorado Springs, Col.: NavPress, 2004).

10. William J. Federer, *America's God and Country* (Coppell, Tex.: FAME Publishing, Inc., 1996), 93.

11. Ibid., 97.

12. Ibid., 96.

13. Ibid., 98.

14. Junes Hines Moore, *Manners Made Easy* (Nashville, Tenn.: Broadman & Holman Publishers, 2001), 4.

15. Stanton, *My Crazy Imperfect Christian Family,* 178.

16. John Kirk Rosemond, "Living with Children," (1998), 2.

17. When he was a toddler, my nephew dubbed my very well-mannered mother "Ma."

Chapter 7

1. Hank Ketcham, "Dennis the Menace" Syndicated Comic Strip, 21 March 2004.

2. Marvin Olasky, "Is America Undergoing a Religious Revival?" *The Wall Street Journal,* 20 March 1998, W13.

3. Bill Fancher, "Expert Hails Homeschooling as American Family's Great Hope," (22 March 2004), found online at www.lifeway.com/lwc/ article_main_page/0%2C1703%2CA%253D156617%2526M%253D20013 1%2C00.html.

4. Chris Klicka, *Home Schooling: The Right Choice* (Nashville, Tenn.: Broadman & Holman Publishers, 2002), 415.

5. Allan Carlson,Ph.D., "How Homeschooling Strengthens Families," a speech to the Alaska Private and Home Educators Association Convention in Anchorage, Alaska (17 April 1998), found online at www.pro fam.org/docs/acc/thc_acc_hhssf.htm.

6. Sam B. Peavey, Ed.D., from "Observations and Perspectives on Home Education" prepared for the Iowa State Board of Education, (5 August 1989), 2.

7. Nancy Vogel, *Robert Frost, Teacher* (Bloomington, Ind.: Phi Delta Kappa, 1974), 7.

8. Ibid., 62.

9. Gatto, *A Different Kind of Teacher,* 40.

10. This quote from the Ben Lippen newsletter was part of an article by Kathy Carper in *The SCAIHS Advantage* (Winter 2001, Year 11, Issue 3), 1, 14.

11. Jane M. Healy, Ph.D., *Endangered Minds,* 131.

12. Zan Tyler, "What Should Your Child's Classroom Look Like?" *The Homeschool Source E-newsletter,* (5 May 2004), found online at www.life way.com/homeschool.

13. Nancy Vogel, *Robert Frost,* 26.

14. *100 Top Picks for Homeschool Curriculum* can be found at www.life way.com/homeschool.

15. A list of state homeschool organizations can be found at www.life way.com/homeschool.

16. You can find more information about the South Carolina Association of Independent Home Schools at www.scaihs.org. Other contact information is 930 Knox Abbott Drive, Cayce, SC 29033; phone (803) 454-0427; E-mail: scaihs@scaihs.org.

17. Margaret B. Pumphrey, *Stories of the Pilgrims* (Arlington Heights, Ill.: Christian Liberty Press, 1991), 149.

18. For information on KONOS curriculum, visit them online at www.konos.com or contact them at KONOS, Inc., P.O. Box 250, Anna, Texas, 75409, (972) 924-2712.

19. Noah Webster knew twenty-eight languages by the time he wrote the first American dictionary published in 1828. He also wrote American text-books on a wide variety of subjects.

20. *Noah Webster's First Edition of an American Dictionary of the English Language.* Reprinted in 1995 by the Foundation for American Christian Education. This information is actually garnered from an introductory article by Rosalie Slater entitled "Noah Webster, Founding Father of American Scholarship and Education," page 10.

21. Gatto, *A Different Kind of Teacher,* 16–17.

22. Nancy Vogel, *Robert Frost,* 49.

23. Ibid., 7.

24. See www.brainyquote.com/quotes/w/walterscott100878.html.

Chapter 8

1. "The Book of Daniel," *The New Open Study Bible* (Nashville, Tenn.: Thomas Nelson Publishers, 1990), 941.

2. John C. Maxwell, *The 21 Irrefutable Laws of Leadership* (Nashville, Tenn. Thomas Nelson Publishers, 1998), 139.

3. Ibid., 219.

4. Ibid.

Appendix

1. The majority of this story first appeared in *Anyone Can Homeschool* by Dr. Terry Dorian and Zan Tyler (Lafayette, La.: Huntington House Publishers, 1996), 21–25, 68–70.

2. For more information on HSLDA, visit them online at www.hslda.org.

3. Zan Tyler, "South Carolina Home Schoolers Celebrate Legislative Victory," *The Home School Court Report,* 8, no. 3, May/June 1992 (Purcellville: Home School Legal Defense Association), 3.

4. For more information, visit SCAIHS online at www.scaihs.org.

5. Steve Suits, Jim Carper, John Watson, and I were all SCAIHS board members.